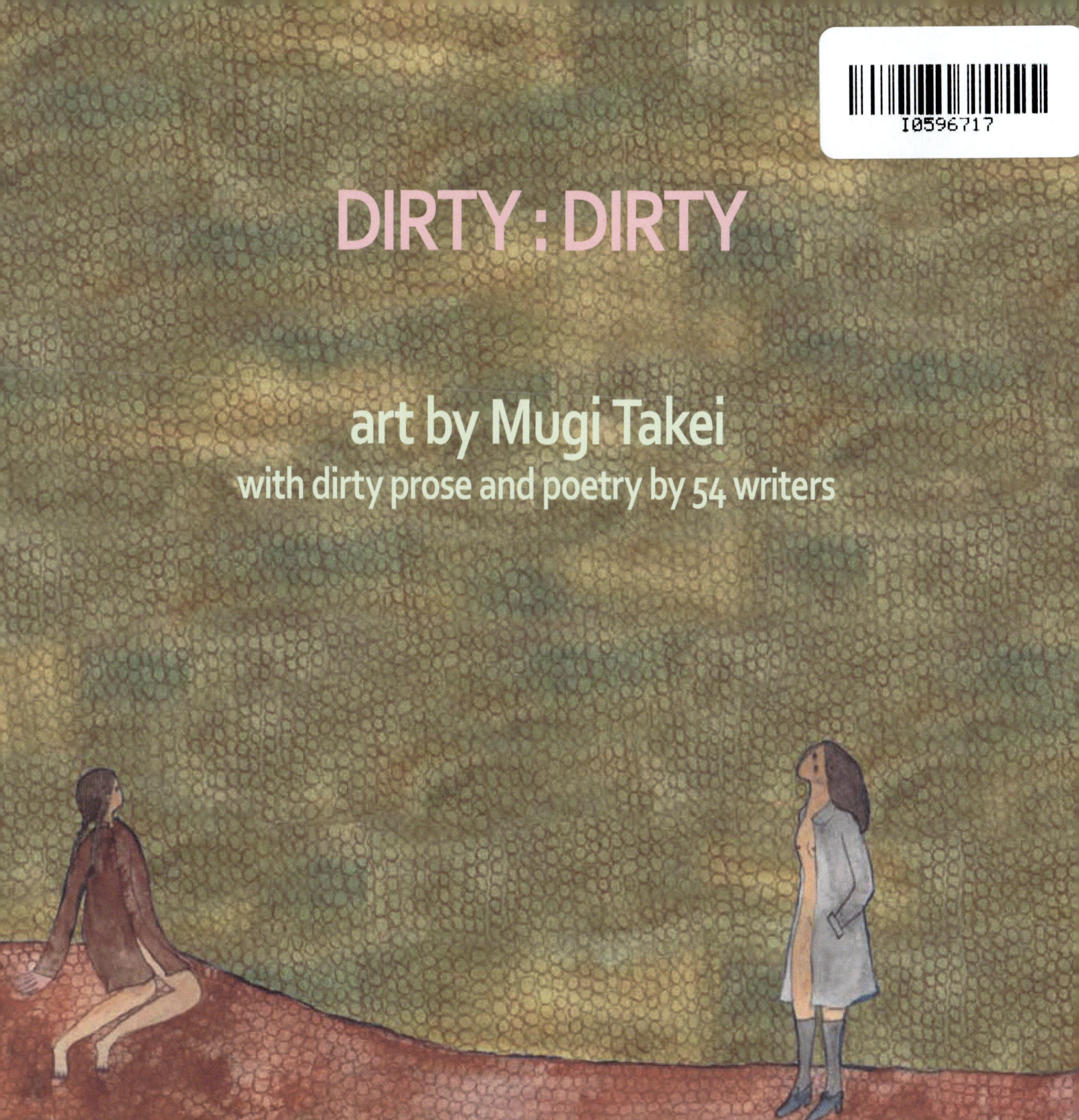

# DIRTY : DIRTY

## art by Mugi Takei
with dirty prose and poetry by 54 writers

# DIRTY : DIRTY

## art by Mugi Takei
### with dirty prose and poetry by 54 writers

**Jaded Ibis Press**
sustainable literature by digital means™
**an imprint of Jaded Ibis Productions U.S.A.**

# TABLE OF CONTENTS

# PREFACE

It's pleasant being naked, as swimmer or writer or reader. On a beach in the Antilles one can frolic bare-ass among exposed skins of all ages — toddlers to octogenarians — and fat to thin, black to white, and shapes and hues between and beyond. Water does not discriminate. Sand burns equally hot for all. Do words?

Marie Antoinette, for all her immodest spending, bathed with her clothes on.

Naked's a way of being free, unencumbered by garment or censor. There exists no other way of knowing certain things, or oneself, without stripping away.

One afternoon on Cupecoy Beach in St. Maarten, when the waves were breaking ten feet high, a man in his seventies body-surfed naked, repeatedly beaching himself, cock-down, onto the sand until I thought he must surely have flayed what foreskin remained. But he was happy. No, he was *exhuberant*. He laughed as he clambered to his feet, threw his hands victoriously into the air and hooted, and then headed right back into the water to catch another wave.

I was young then. And he must be dead by now.

If life's indeed a beach then the waves are words tumbling us onto hot sand: *surf or drown*. There is no dirt.

— Debra Di Blasi, Editor

Here we go, my cock in your mouth, your head in my pussy, one leg out the window, the other steering madly across the gossamer bridges of the Pennsylvania turnpike. You pull out the camera and hike my skirt. I'm talking to you, gorgeous. You've got my hands tied but I can still call directions. Right, left, dangerous curves ahead. Animal parts fly into the backseat. The camera shudders. Photos of unkempt sacrificial mounds upload instantly via space brains. A thousand views this minute, a movie deal the next. Your hands weave the wind through the sunroof. Our lips part and resume. The mountain eats us into her tunnel and shits us, sweating, out her lush and muddy anus. I can't thank you enough, dear, for lending us the Chrysler with the Corinthian leather and cruise control. Over the hills and through the woods; three knuckles deep and pumping pistons until there's no nothing, nada. You lick into my ear: your meow meow meows, your Sweet wet baby, you gonna die, blow your stack on my titties and don't ask why. By the way you're rolling your tongue, I take you seriously. In fact, I'm scared half there but here we come, oh oh oh over the rainbow, over the top, over the curbside railing into the gaping valley below, exploding a gazillion bajillion sparks into the dreams of trailing truckers. The one with the mutton chops toots his horn. He knows it's a big lie. We live on. Just close your eyes and gently google our name.

mikal shapiro

*"...feel that shit all up in your body."* –Miles Davis

When he's in his groove: riff'n on his licks, blow'n through the changes: the tempo & timbre he trusts to be true:

That when his sax touches the deepest, seminal spot in her, the slit at the end of his cock opens to kiss the same way her pussy lips do, the syzygy of their most private wet & salty hearts reverberating pressed together.

That there are a variety of melodious flavors waiting unsung inside her, from the first silky lube to the musk of her ass to a furtive heady cream deep down, only reached when he plumbs her by tonguing subtone & with his cock's funky back beat.

That her vagina can feel & remember & mold around & preserve the shape of his shaft & glans, like the neck & flared bell of his sax glinting in the dark.

That her clit is a petite penis with an aperture of its own that will gush astonishing cum, a Siren solo with a spontaneous essence he is wild to savor.

That the head of the tune, the elemental melody, the only part narrated in written notes, is just an excuse to get going & see what happens.

cris mazza

#1: Never trim body hair while holding your favorite dildo. But if you absolutely must, make sure to sit down first.

#2: He. Is. A. Monster. Just lie still until I'm home.

#3: Glen Campbell is a great lay; you don't need a copy of Playgirl to tell you that.

#4: Cable television will rob you of your soul. The Food Network is the only proof I'll ever need to back that up. Have you seen Diners, Drive-Ins and Dives? I worked at the Depot Grill for nearly 40 years and no one ever filmed jack-shit there. The closest thing I ever saw to a camera there was when Mister Soran brought in his Polaroid Instamatic, but you're not nearly old enough to hear that story.

#5: Officially, your grandfather died of a heart attack. I guess.

#6: Your uncle used to wait up for me when I went out on dates. He wanted to make sure I always made it home okay so he would sneak into my room after Mom put him to bed and thought he was asleep. You remind me a lot of him even though...well...you know.

#7: When someone says "I love you," you have their implicit permission to beat them within inches of their life. Seriously. Watch.

#8: Never write anything long-hand except grocery lists and the checks you use to pay your bills. Nothing else is so damn important that you have to show yourself naked like that.

#9: Go ahead and pick out anything you want in the house. You can have it after I'm dead and sell it or whatever you like. I am having you do this now because I need to know how much you think you value me. C'mon now. I have to get to work.

trevor dodge

CC Shaboom, the virgin slut

CC tryin            lookin   looking

CC with a fro, with a Princess Layya, with the pigtails low, ponytail high, with lemon juice and peroxide, with Clairol

CC to dye, to die, with a Di

CC do-ya-wanna  hava a tongue in your ear

a hand down your pants, down the back, down the front

CC you-wanna, you-know-you-wanna,    Want It

CC do-ya-know

CC do-ya-wanna  have a tongue in       have a cock in

NO              No            no            n      o

CC by a candle or camp fire or burning building, by the hand inching in   the cock crowing   the cunt crying

CC do-ya-wanna

CC with nipples the size of quarters, of dollars, of tuna cans

CC happy as an eraser, as a pin, as a pen, or was that whorror


jane carman

**GHOSTS**

When all is ending, you find yourself sending text messages to a 19 year old in California that read "I need you to come in my mouth" and "I want us to fuck each other to sleep." He will write back with "Yes." And "We will," will call you "lover" and "shadow." While there is not much more to be said, you will continue to say it. Your mouth spills words like salt. When all is ending, you are wet for days. It is summer. Your body and your cunt drip and don't stop. You are overflowing. You compare the boy to a river, and he doesn't thank you. Instead, he talks about incest, says he will make you call him "brother." You don't know how to pronounce his real name, so you never say it.

You no longer say your real lover's name. You speak the A, soft and drawn out, and leave the rest, pretend you can dislocate him from the word. You have heard that speaking a demon's name gives it power. You still fuck him, stretching to reach his mouth in the middle of the night when it is easier to forget his face. Your body is lighter, quicker on top of his. You are a different person than you were, a shadow. You move in and out of doorways and don't remember how you got there. When you open your mouth, what comes out is less than smoke.

**SNOW**

When all has ended, you make plans for a 45-year-old in Berlin to stay with you in December. You have an apartment of your own now, in the country. Your first night there, you sobbed and begged your ex-lover not to leave you there by yourself. You kissed him, thought about fucking him on the

beth couture

mattress on your living room floor, but you both fell asleep instead. Now you are friends with your neighbors and feel peaceful sometimes, though just as often you sit on the porch and smoke and cry. You drive slowly down your road at night, worried about deer and falling rocks, and at night you hear crickets and tree frogs. You wonder if they are mating, if they have made families, babies they'll abandon once they are able to crawl. Stephen—you say his name easily—says he wants to see the winter where you are, wants to back you up against a tree in the snow. He tells you to get used to the way ice feels on your bare skin. He says your body is his, and you agree but don't know what that means. You make yourself come every time you talk to him, but it's not him you're thinking about. You aren't sure who it is, though you can smell him on your body for hours after.

RIPE

You talk yourself into things. You eat fruit that isn't ripe—peaches that taste cold and bland, rubbery mangoes. You slice and peel them and try to feel sensual, sexy, as you bite into their flesh. You imagine a man watching you from your window, standing in the yard and touching himself to the sight of you with fruit in your mouth. You think about touching yourself too, in the kitchen and living room, in the shower, but you wait until bedtime. You do it quietly, though what you want is to scream, to make noises like animals. Even now you hold back. You try not to think about what this means. You think about your ex-lover, about sex with him, and you imagine him eating mangoes with the girl who now loves him, the juice dripping down their chins. You throw all the fruit in your refrigerator away and then fish it out later and wash it in cold water. None of it matters, you say, and sometimes you believe it but most of the time you're sure it does. It all matters more than you ever thought it could.

1. with alchemic attention, Geoff and James tried to make love in the bathtub like love was crystal meth: cheap, illegal, labor intensive and so the whole god damned neighborhood could smell it.

2. childhood nostalgia of spitting into promised palms-- shaking them into unbreakable bonds --inspired Jonathan and Rebecca to fold frictional flesh upon itself until it was impossible to tell who was who--- what was bush, what was beard. lying there until congealed fluids held them tight like old promises beyond the point either wanted the other's secrets.

3. after reading Pygmalion, Paul unspooled outdated VHS porn to duct-tape into the visage of every woman therein--- a chimera accomplishing everything but conversation.

4. led by the example of parents, Mary and David attempted to forge love out of metal bands and were still astonished when it failed them as it did their parents.

5. Gwen and Stacy tried to make it out of words. foundation built by pleasantries. first floor formed by stated love with windows where passion left things unsaid. second floor the same but without windows; only a fire escape. third floor sits lopsided--- one side refusing growth as the other pulls overused words from below to try to jenga it into something monumental.

6. made from faulty mechanics-- clockwork of premature precision --by Ray and Laurie for forty years until the former cog cracked and batteries provided a sustained alternative to the last lonely years of lovelessness.

7. with pioneering spirit, Brenda and Rob bungeed comforter corners to the bed frame to make thrusts a series of failed escapes and forced recoils back to this world. it wasn't any better. both too tired to escape the bonds Monday morning, waiting for work to call wondering where they were.
8. Anastasia used spoons and a decorative rock.

c.vance

9. then there was Jenny who tried to make it from things left behind mornings after failed cooperative attempts: shellacked condoms scraped from hardwood floors, stale smells, cigarette butts, stripped buttons and bad-breath goodbyes of someday-soon statements. all compiled into an altar trying to remember one unified good someone out of so many nameless nobodies.

10. the etched flesh of Carrie and Vincent not only bloodied sheets but proclaimed unreasonable demands. demands like:
   —Uncompromise with only your left side like a stroke victim.
   —Hum a pop song with me in your mouth.
   —Sparkle.
   documented in scars to forever remember in case one unreasonable action felt like love made.

11. a mistake was made by Harold and Cherice; kept and mislabeled Love.

12. another Jonathan convinced Allison to drunkenly try and coerce love to rise from them-- accompanied by a chorus of horns --in streets where nothing reaches higher than fast food signs scraped by steeples.

13. they thought they had it, Stella and Andy, but wanted to manufacture better by penetrating each other with objects loved: antique china dolls, power tools, her grandfather's lopsided armoire's leg, microbrew bottles... on and on until they became these things and were no longer the self the other originally had.

14. we tried with chemical stimulants, mail order enhancements and marathoned attempts through cramped muscles and lack of lube; self-made or otherwise. we tried through screams, through wailed Hank Williams songs, through the silence our bodies broke in collision. we tried in barroom bathrooms, high school dugouts, library bookshelves and Sunday morning pews. we tried and tried and tried and failed--- but that never stopped us from enjoying the process.

I

The man tells the boy that most men like to put their penises inside women because women have a lovely receptacle where they house men's penises. This has been the way since time immemorial, he says. But now some men like to put their penises inside other men, he says.

The boy looks at the man.

It's true, the man says.

Why is this the case, Daddy, the boy says.

Because they have been bamboozled, the man says.

Bamboozled?

Yes, son. Bamboozled up the asshole. Someone did this to them when they were little and this is what happens.

Did anyone ever bamboozle you, Daddy?

No, son. And no one is going to bamboozle you, either.

How do you know?

I just know it, son. Don't worry.

I don't think I want to be bamboozled.

No one does, son.

But you said most men like to put their penises inside women, right?

That's right.

Do most men have more than one penis? Because I have only the one.

No son, most men have only one penis. Almost everyone, I think.

So no one has more than one penis?

I think I've seen it once or twice – a man with more than one penis. But it's rare.

Have they been bamboozled? Is that why?

I don't know the medical reason, son. But it wouldn't surprise me.

II

One of them says pussy's pussy and he looks at the other. It's a kind of challenge.

The other says pussy is not pussy. Decidedly, he says.

The first of them says, then what is it then?

The second says you have to open your eyes. It's obvious, he says.

The first says this is where you are wrong. He says, pussy is always pussy.

robert lopez

In those early days we noticed the connection between pleasure and pain. A rub or a pinch brings the same effect: tiny pink mound bursts forth as if to say "more, more!" It's all relative; suck or nip, all the brain registers is feel. But then the line (ah, the line) gets crossed, and now it's all tangled up. I can't get wet without the slap; you can't get off without the punch. Bite, thrust, claw, grind. As we become intertwined, nothing matters anymore except stimulus and reaction. Soon we don't look like lovers but victims. The post-coital glow replaced by the post-coital bruise and bandage. I wear you like a badge. If you break my skin, that brings you closer to being inside me.

For those few moments we are teeth and tongues and fingernails and cock all seeking the ultimate penetration.

jacqueline heffron

The first time 3 did it was at her apartment.

It is summer in Fresno, and even the night air is hot. 1 tell her about my six-month girlfriend whom 1 had never kissed. Her eyes soften as her head moves closer. She kisses me, he kisses me, and all 3 kiss one another.

2 had spoken of this happening, but had never believed it actually would.

[flashback]

A week prior, he had taken she and me to get our navels pierced.. 3 went back to the house 2 shared and got drunk. She ended up sleeping on the couch, so 2 made love with the door open, hoping she would hear us.

[/flashback]

3 nude bodies, a blanket on the floor, a burning candle. 2 proceeded to caress her to orgasm; after, he fucked her while 1 played with her tits. 1 fucked him as she watched and touched herself. All the while, the room spun and shimmered with candlelight; 1 succumbed to it, then 3 came.

The morning after wasn't awkward. 3 were nakedly discussing what had been done, giggling all the while. Then 3 got dressed and went to Denny's.

[2 year triad]

Memories of her, memories of us, memories of 3 and the many moments shared, are snippets from a powdery-pink towel, too stiffened with semen and stained with vodka to be of any use. 2 run away from in hopes of something better.

[/2 year triad]

alyssa wisener

embedded between your ink-wet nights and molten days, you, sacred tree, under my arm and circling, lunar, humid and carved from (my) small breaths /

you sweep herbs beneath the bed, across our skin, decapitate love, installation of comets, their dust trailing our night like lonely specters, your hair, lassoed by my fists and flowing in waves, eternity fragmented in the promise /into shards of /into the smallest of units /(like cells, we multiply by colonizing each other)

cannibalized, you reach inside yourself quiver look into the night of me your never ending body flattened, as if traced on paper, our edges pressed together (elbows, knees), this tempest could pull me up by my roots, you, wrap around me, a helix penned across my skin pulped and bludgeoned with lips, pinches, crushing, sad transition to a fragmented lust lather of soprano screaming soft as mud regress and, without more, without magic, you arc in galvanic currents

you form an "o" with your lips, divine articulation transformed in mental middles a molecular melancholy cardinal combustion, sky / skin / vellum, impenetrable pigments leaden and leaning in wet rushes maturing birdcalls, howls open me, the night fissures, you, murmuring, fuming, ready to harvest yourself, your hands your fingers discover a lost flesh purified by biting and you, falling from my mouth a lamplight away, beyond sleep in the discolored light you shape, you who never sleeps, shifting under black sheets, wringing the pillowcase

if i sing you to sleep if i lick your wounds, salt, crush scars with my lips until their memory is mine, the tip of my tongue becomes knowing you, your flesh takes its toll on me

laura vena

A naked man moves in on his homemade bride. Her crudely constructed exoskeleton of metal piping wrapped in pink duct-tape lays sprawled on the floor, legs spread to reveal a huge mutilated rat, legs and tail amputated, eyes stabbed out, mouth cleared of teeth. Bound to the makeshift coccyx with copper wiring, it palpitates like a furry heart. His face, made up with colouring pens, is reflected in hers: a hand-mirror rammed into the top of her spinal column, lengths of red and white flex glued to its plastic frame. He kisses her lips, pressing down hard, their tongues locked in harmonious struggle: a defeated echo wrestling against itself. Soon tiring of the niceties, he rams it home, straight through into those squirming contours (ribbed for his pleasure), displacing blood and organs with every stroke. Having fucked the rat dry he begins sobbing, his tears forming multicoloured pools on her bevel-edged cheek-bones.

My guide speaks: "Such are the maggot-marrowed bones of lust; such are the trappings of love."

Through an open door I watch a party of fleshy metronomes. The puzzled detail of their faces belies the smooth, patterned order of their encounter. A vagina breaks free of its repeated union, pulsating grotesquely like a garroted throat. There are joints in her laughter where some damaged humanity might have resided if there'd been a poet present to give it dignity; instead the silent seams are filled with snorts, the sliding of nooses, and electrodes sucking on loose skin. A man fingers the grey dough of her gut, his damaged gaze made up of old fragments of a distant explosion. An un-owned smile creeps up her cheeks.

My guide speaks: "They're in a loop. They'll be there for days. They'll be there till there's nothing left."

I decide to wait.

gary j. shipley

I thought she would want me to direct things, that's how our friendship had been, but immediately she said lay down on the mattress. I did it. Her voice was calm and quiet. She said take off your pants, your shirt. I did it. Sweat formed on my upper lip simply from her asking me to do ordinary things. Language. Lie down.

A whisper of heat fluttered the hotel white linen curtain. Glimpse of cerulean. A truck rolling by miles from our lives.

She said touch yourself. Soft. Pelt. She said close your eyes. I heard the first click of the camera. She said squeeze the sweet meat of your pussy until you are wet. I did. That's when I felt her eye on me close in—the lens of her. She said milk your tits. I did. My mouth opening barely. The camera clicking.

She said take off your panties. Alive skin.

She said whatever you do, don't open your eyes again. I don't. Everything becomes present and past tense, like in a photo.

I squeeze the full palmed whole of each breast and knead them upward. Swollen. I pinch my nipples. Reddening. Mouthable. Laden. The camera clicking like sparks. Her moving in and out. I said I've never done this. I mean like this. Hipbones ache arching.

Whisper white curtain.

Hum of diesel.

I move my hands down to my cunt. She said pull your pussy lips apart first and show me. She said show me your clit, I want to see your swollen clit. I do it. I drive my hips toward her voice. I think I hear her use a zoom. I fuck the air showing her my clit and my wide open pussy, as slowly as possible. A throbbing.

She said shhhh. Small mechanical device at the mouth of me. She said hold very still. I am taking your picture.

Outside a desert. Wetted.

lidia yuknavitch

we love

A boy's life had been taken at Clynnyd, at the green sea. The boy had been three years old and drowned. At sunrise everyone from the town came—we stood behind the policemen's line. We never let the sheep out that morning and the animals cried in the barns. The boy's mother was not to be seen; maybe she had been enfolded by a group of women who stood on the stone hill. I could not tell—I had to look away.

What to do but sit with it? You don't recover from this. I did not want to face the boy's mother again, not even across the distance of the sea road.

The town's cabinetlike kitchens with latticed roofs released stove smoke and the drinking men were crying, leaning on walls. I approached the group of women up the pebbly hill. The mother was not there. The children played on the boulders nearby, cruelly, as if nothing had happened.

Norman and Selmer stood on the hill too. I knew I shouldn't touch Norman, for the children weren't so young now and understood sexuality very well, though they had not yet sought it for themselves.

But Norman looked at me and I went to him. His stolid appearance and protruding eyes were unappealing, yet my revulsion made me hungrier. While the gray-sweatered women wept, I clawed him along his front. He was weak from the day and slid down. We clawed each other with mouths. As the raw feeling over came my eyes, Selmer, who was brain-injured and narrated everything he saw, honked, "Marie and Norman are taking each other!"

This is Clynnyd. Every few days or so in this town, you realize your life is nowhere like secure, and that you are still waiting for money, comfort, and ease.

stacey levine

I        kind        of              hope
                          you              will
       break my nose
                 s      o
               your lips  will      taste           like
       iron
             and     I     won't  have  to
                    bite                 you
             till      you                    bleed
with  your  knee            at  my  face
                               fucking          lazily
but          you're     the  jack-rabbit          type
        so          maybe        if          I am
here      long enough
                   your kneecap        will crush
       the cartilage
                     &                      bone
               of      my  nose

and        I will  taste      the  taste      you  taste  where
          you  lick          my
                          vagina    which
no     longer          bleeds


       kimberly koga

Tad Waller sat naked on the edge of a small green Victorian chair in the corner of his spacious bedroom. In the defused light from his reproduction Tiffany dragonfly lamp he stared at his fifty-nine year-old limp white dick and painfully, but honestly contemplated his future sex life. The future did not seem to hold much promise. Several years before, quite suddenly, sufficient amounts of blood no longer flowed into his penis. It could happen, a really good hard on, but not in the normal course of things. To make his old dick stand tall he needed excessive forms of stimulation. He'd peer into his wife's open wet pussy, push two or three fingers inside, and extract some of her magic elixir, rubbing the silky mélange into his dick. This often did the trick, but Tad was only too aware that it was a trick. Perhaps saving his sex life was just too convoluted. Perhaps he should just let the whole thing go. After all, if he were freed from insistent desire it would be for the first time in his life, at least since he reached puberty, a time when self-abuse came naturally and often. What really scared him was how easy it would be to just give it up. He rationalized he'd get more work done; he'd have more time for grandchildren and friends. But, he'd dedicated so much of his life to the pursuit of women's sexual favors that not having intercourse seemed a kind of premature death. Was it all then, just a love of the game? For some men, acceptance might be easy, even a relief, one might say cleverly, a release, but Tad loved having sex. For him sex had always been what football had been to Vince Lombardi. Sex wasn't the best thing, it was the only thing. Quietly, Tad dressed and remembered Aesop's insight, "We would be sorry if our wishers were gratified." Tad hoped it was a question.

hal wert

Nothing but a plug of wet blood exploding from my cunt.

My cunt is a vacuum, and your fingers fall deep into the dry hole.

On the edge of my cunt lips, your fingers absorb the fleshy brack of my pussy, and then, suddenly, your arm falls deep into the floating vagina, its length swallowed as a supercharged catheter hose snaking through my intestine in search of a cancerous polyp.

My cunt throbs with each articulated syllable.

My cunt is soooo satisfied by the shapes of your mouth: the wondrous O pursing lips, the intoxicating spell of the M pulling my upper lip slightly over its bottom as a crippled insect might be sewn into the white spin of a spiderweb.

The room spins like a circular train track running through the same middle-class living space, and it's all you can do to keep from falling unconscious under the enormous Christmas tree of my cunt.

You run your hand into the lubricated sweet of my asshole as your tongue corrodes over the open eyeball of my cunt covered in fluttering lash and you taste my vision in a boiling soup of nervous shimmers while the hot eyeball explodes into a candy sun, endlessly foaming your tongue and your breath.

You read transmogrified surface patterns around my useless cunt of an eye with your own burnt fingers.

My cunt shivers as if bursting apart.

Your lips are cracked and dry from the ooze of my starched-up cunt.

You speak through my cunt in the language of desire.

No, I didn't know you hated gladiolus because you say it reminds you of a penis split into many smaller pieces and rimmed around my dried-up cunt.

So hold on tight, my ill- nurtured cunt ball, you're finally going to do me some good.

davis schneiderman

Then consequence. Then perish. Then seed. Then want. If my future is no longer fixed, certain. If I was once evolving. Then what. Can we label this. What name to give this. How shall we pin it. What specimen. What Latinate. What genus.

If perversion is a consequence of degeneration, then first I must know if this is perversion. Or evolving. Then. If this is a coming back to the body, then let it be a coming. Let it. A regression to the body to taste to moisture sweat and smell. Copper on the tongue and the bitter throat.

If it is the body's last efforts to fruit. Like too dry plants shoot out their flowers on their journey to the death, last hope. Then yes. Then render this body transparent. Reduce me to its simple cells and vessels. The heart. The cunt. The brain. The anus. The mouth. The life cycle of the nine-day worm. Does the nematode worm desire. Does she prey. Does she worship the body and her transparent skin.

If this desire whose functions have not yet been determined. Then tease it out for me. Each gene. Each broken leg of the ladder. Infer each probable function. Observe the grind. Research the watering mouth. Grant funds for the moan into his collarbone.

kylee cook

There were notches in the headboard, the dents in the walls behind flaked deep.

Toes curled. The chorus sang sore for hours afterwards.

All accounts made payable to Pro Bono Gigalo LLC, a private enterprise for the greater good.

Old Greek couple next door banged on the walls when primal screams reached past their game shows.

He claimed that this was his testified restitution for thousands of years of unchecked patriarchy and all that. Utter servitude and bouts of hysterical paroxysm.

Goddess Venus in furs blurs churning surprise smile gag laugh grunt hump slap.

Words spoken in reverse, a broom to cleanse the room after, tip dipped, spiritual fragment of a satyr dangled into her angle, smeared wiped globbed nutriment onto an altar by the bed, humming, buzzing, island fertility hips like Gauguin's dreamtime with sweaty heads, beads of sweat pooled on flesh young and old, warped and regal, wrinkled and glowing smooth, all the same, he said to them, all is One, warm entrance and exit, with fire and water forming the steam of this new age, ushered in by generous tumescence.

More. Harder. Deeper.

They had deep personal revelations, shuddering after hours of work.

Chapped lips and zits licked. Stretch marks and deep wrinkles kissed.

lane williams

He offered himself advice with imaginary post-its on various parts at certain points, each Hera, each Juno, each Aphrodite. Each Eris.

Lick here.

Stroke here like a butterfly,

here like a hummingbird,

bite this like a horse-fly.

Pinch, flick, flip.

More is never enough.

He found himself, in the buzz of the room afterward, kicking at sticky lost panties constantly underfoot, dancing as if televised.

Bathed with the blue glow of the altar, a stale cigarette stink stuck to everything as he drifted into dreams of endless curvatures.

The old squaw sat hunched over, reliving what she had encountered long ago, but what seemed to be so fresh in her memory:

"I had the dirt of the creek loosely pulled in around me, hiding and holding myself as tightly as I clenched my eyes shut. Yet the images were burned in solid, and the darkness of my eyelids were no sanctuary from this mess that was all around me. I saw breasts, testicles, and various genitalia ripped from their rightful owners and taken as souvenirs by the snarling, intoxicated men. Some body parts were used as tobacco pouches. Others, such as labia, were stretched across and used as hat bands. Unborn children were also hanging from their hats as they boasted of their courageousness. I recall women being thrust upon some time after their spirits had escaped from their ravaged bodies....their blood mingling with the seeds of the beasts. We had even displayed two flags: their striped flag and a white flag. In the end, they were covered in the splattered remains of my tribesmen. The former preacher and his men hung the dripping pieces of my people up at the Denver theater as though they were trophies for all to see. I'm sorry for speaking of such dreadful things..."

I sat still for a moment, feeling nausea creep in.

"Please do not apologize," I said. "It's not your words that are offensive but rather the vulgarity of history itself."

*(Fictional conversation based upon factual events of the massacre at Sand Creek)*

heather hendrix russell

The rest of the passengers on the aircraft, all of whom we're surprised to learn are women, must, the flight attendant says on our behalf, take off their pants and skirts, and now their shirts, followed by the bra and those panties, so that when everyone's sitting in their seats naked, we foist Flight Attendant up (her flight attendant's cap having been knocked off during the initial scuffle, her blonde locks fall in big, pull-able bunches), spinning her torso mid-air so that her legs point straight up, likened here to two golden fireplace tongs that we now spread in order to run our tongue along the folds of her vagina, periodically nibbling away at her nerve center, momentarily stopping to command Flight Attendant to reciprocate, which she does at first hesitantly and in great fear (she must do it to save the other passengers, nevertheless), and voila, a standing 69—hence the title— although, thusly engaged, we still frequently eye the other passengers suspiciously, we're informed, but they, too, are becoming aroused (evidently our point of view reveals that there's lots of lip licking among them), so we wave the gun (evidently, we've been in possession of a gun), telling the now dopey-eyed Flight Attendant to translate (translate?) you American sluts, you get fucking, and that's all it takes, apparently, because there's a sudden swarm of groping, a fuckfest at 30,000 feet, someone offers, citing the description as possible promotional copy, which, particularly as we're beginning to run short on time—to say nothing of the fact that the decision of whether or not we really want pursue actual production, as opposed to just distribution is still a source of hot debate— provides an opportune segue to the other, related item on the agenda: "Trends Analysis."

christopher grimes

My Kimchi's fermented anchovy laser stink eye skips click tracks like Zaxxon zaps skip levels to motherbase. I cannot re-corral the reefs of her vulvic coral from Al Gore's global warning. I could hunt her cunt unto a besmirched glacier or the besotted offal of my affections tumble into the drinkfat of her oceanic tabloid breast reduction leftovers warming in the ozonal microwave. Her Medusa-coif fangs my vellumed face & even pockmarks her mandibles, maxillae, & jowls covered o'er with melanoma & the half-ingested scrota, foreskins, & testes of late flings. A landfill molotov tang of methane, sperm, & urea seeps from her rump & a rotted olive stink creeps from her toothsome beek, but oh! the souring geranium stank of her sebaceous woman pit, a potter's field glazed with smegma, or her tit pits teeming with yeasty wee beasties. And the secret siren song of her underarm propionibacteria wafting bromhidrosis (also called osmidrosis & ozochrotia, or known as fetid sweat, body smell, & malodorous sweating). I fly-shit to her nasally bellows & entreaties, & her phlegmatic hacks, yawps, & hawks yield blood-dotted tubercular loogie sputum, which I, as promethean raptor in nightly mechanized glory simulation, devour, regurge, & redevour devoutly. I never saw any bag lady or street carp scratch & squeeze at an anorexic forearm's open sores, but if pus is what's for dinner then I'll dip a googolplex of scabies, lice, & crabs into her pyogenic bacterial infections, eat deep & dream none other.

steve halle

I only like the one bakery. It's not far from my house, so I walk there every day. I begin walking early in the morning, just as the sun is minting the treetops, and take it slow. Very early along in my walk I cross a high wooden bridge that hangs over a comically little stream and across from the bridge is an engraved sign which is always changing, and today it tells me about Gertrude. There is much to know about Gertrude. She lives in a cabin not far from there. She is a grandmother, but not very old. Her thighs are creamy and I would be sexually attracted to her, so much that I would like to embrace her straight away.

It is not far up the path where a bed of straw is and there I must take a nap as the hill to the bakery is so steep, and while I nap I dream of the bakery. It's run by a tall woman and her three children, Alice, Robert, and Nellie. Nellie is oldest. Her hair is parted in the middle, but meets again with a magical braid in the back. Nellie's a renagade baker. She makes a savory that's only for me, that makes me sexually wild, yet it's not she who gets the mountains of cream sprayed in her mouth.

justin dobbs

The cop holds the gun to her head and asks her one last time, "Where's the money?" "What money?" He hits her with the gun. "Lying bitch!" She's bleeding at the lips but takes a leisurely moment to lick it, eyes glaring. This turns him on. "How many times do you have sex with those bastards?" She feels the barrel of the gun digging deeper into her skull. "Well, I wouldn't call it sex, I would rather call it fucking." "Damn whore..." he says as his cock gets harder. He pulls the trigger and she collapses onto the bed as if she's dead, but tomorrow she'll play the CEO and he'll be the politician.

helen tran

Before now, it had only been dreamt and joked about, surely. Then there was the sniffing and the smelling, but still, no touching. Next, it was squeezed, poked then prodded by his very own, until the courage was built enough to proceed and penetrate her very own. No one on Earth will ever know what was being said. To me, it sounded like grunting. But this was a conversation. It was an exchange of lustful maneuvers and, at first awkward, then passionate, pauses. They were already what we would consider sullied or dirty, but now they were entering absolute filth. Fluids, juices, blood and hairs, feces from all the early touching and sniffing, became paint. It was everywhere. They had painted the Earth, the inside of their mountain, and each other. One dominated the other. I waited for sounds of submission. But it never came, for the submissive party enjoyed her handling. Their language at this moment was heavy breath and the clapping of flesh. Not soft flesh, but firm strong flesh, that we as humans save for only our finest specimens. It was the sound of clapping meat, substantial meat, sweet meat. The clap began to slow to a wet sucking sound, then perhaps the smacking of soaked lips. This was the soft flesh: ripe, red, and now raw, a reward. Grunts became groans, becoming moans until they fell silent. Thus, ending my encounter peeping on the Neanderthals.

garrett hayes

*a faceless shift into a world I've barely seen only felt the dark wrath of as it coiled its slimy fingers around my pelvis and pushed with all the strength of its thumbs straight into my uterus*

I dream of falling down stairs or losing wing-power mid-flight. In the dreams I'm tumbling while sucking in my belly, thrilled with images of taut white sundresses and short-shorts and lacy-lined bras. The drop lasts decades. I'm a silvery prune before I wake up, never having met my splattered fate.

There's a ladder that leans against my neighbor's house; it catches the cooled sunlight at 9am and beckons me with trickling sparks. Roof, Roof, Roof. I've checked; it's chained to the ground. I think they suspect me.

*your words miscarried meaning a trough of tissue bathed in less we were dancing on the blue line but you were taking what was there wasn't there something meaning full in my expulsion don't I have the power to as/certain this tempting thought*

holms troelstrup

An Oink from China. Plush, a Hug Me I'm Yours white bear heart. A sea thing. A purple teletubby from Eden. Dinosaur dudes with purple shades. A she-dude and a she-bop. I got the pick. Time for another box. The wash, the dirt, the oil is enough. Now they have to be praised. Line the bodies up. All can be saved. "Aren't you pretty," I say, "yum, yum, girls," but don't look in the eyes. Transfigure the world. Frizzy beauts in caliche mud when the hair and a dress comes off. They go their way, but we get them back. Up canal, they land in pickups in awful heat. Garages speak a different language after this. The box is full. I can say that much. The basket is full. One starts to call "Velma" or "Mama." I go to check. Heads bump. They're hot, the water is hot, the heads are bald. I don't see any boys. Eyes peep over suds. Water clears. Bald heads come out. You get closer, pop the lid. Heads go by. One in her fourth mind. One lost a dress. One gained water weight. Stuffing's out. Holes open up. She drips. The machine goes fast. They take off their clothes. It feels good to bathe. I wish we could have them at our club, eyes closed, heads thrown back to drain. It's what we dream, the way dolls are made.

ae reiff

At the appointed time, Bernice made herself available under the bleachers. She put on cherry lip-gloss and brushed her hair—how little she knew of what teenaged boys really care about! She was wearing a fluffy skirt with little blue eyelets embroidered into flowers, tulips maybe. Below the sweet demeanor, however, she sported a black thong, lace, and she was happy to feel her pubic hair sift around its edges. She thought it was sexy, and it was. Bernice, in anticipation for Johnny, propped the toe of her right foot onto the edge of a bleacher seat, about waist high, moved it back, such that a certain teenaged soccer player, when approaching, could see her pale skin, luminous against the blackness of her panties, obscuring her virgin cunt underneath. Johnny didn't show though. Josef did. Skinny, nerdy Josef, who awkwardly fingered her—more like an excavation than anything pleasurable—while she took his semen in her mouth. And Josef, being a virgin, didn't understand that there was a necessary lag time between orgasms, after coming, demanded to have sex with her, and Bernice, also being a virgin, let him. So pushed against the fake brick wall underneath the bleachers, standing up, Bernice lost her virginity. It took him ages to come again, and Bernice's whimpering only made things more difficult, "harder" being an inappropriate word in this situation, but he did eventually, ejaculate his semen into her vagina, which eventually became Martha. Of course, by the next day, Josef wanted nothing to do with Bernice, called her a "bad lay" and made sure everyone knew about it.

lily hoang

When I cum the shivering and the quickening and the cum shoots from my pussy in a way that has never happened before--like a man's. I cum and I cry. My pussy opens and closes in violent contractions, the dark of the inside of me meeting the light of the white sheets and walls, the production of an image, the intimacy of art, the space between two women, everything balanced in its dark and light.

lidia yuknavitch

The run from the inside of her knee to the inside of her thigh and up to the sweetest tangle of hair and into the pinkest and deepest most beautiful opening lush flesh folds spreading for my tongue, for my mouth, the breath of me, inhaling her against my face, and who was warmer, soft and rolling hips or my following face, and us locked in her rising? This run up to her, this secret trail of my tongue up her leg, I was like a pirate, like a bootlegger, a drug runner. I was after my secrets, and she was waiting for her fix, for me, for the face she cried out for, and couldn't live without.

Her nipples stood and heaved for me.

Her neck arched and her throat released my name again and again.

You tell me how she left.

Tell me how she left.

Someone has to know.

Inside my ribs, something is raining me away.

When I think of him, I think of how he sleeps. I think that when he is next to me he is as long as a sleeping lion. He has eaten of me, eaten and languished and swallowed me and drunk from my throat and loved and wanted and wanted. Until he lay beside me long and wet and warm and cooling. This is him, the way he was, the way he was.

Tell me a potion to get him back.

Finger stuck deep inside, I will go to the edge of the coolth of my longing and scream his name until the curl at the end of the wave of my coming is the dream of his cock and the riding and falling the riding the falling the falling the falling his name his name falling name

elizabeth burns

He wonders why these people insist on wearing dissimilar uniforms. The colors dissatisfy his senses. He wants to tell them about his displeasure, but he doesn't complain anymore. In fact, speaking has not been part of his life for a very long time. He no longer cares what his name is, unless it means that he can go to the gatherings again, where they're herded into a large white room, unfertile and sterile like all the other rooms of this place. He loves a colorless room—clean and easy to spot irregularity. No matter what day or night, women are always in the pale room, looking beyond the windows into the outside. He wants to touch a woman again.

He thinks that women must have liked him once—a thought shortened by age. His physique had always dominated his personality, yet time has exposed his body as a facade to a weedy myopic mind. They, these bastards that wear the un-uniformed uniforms, know he wants women to visit, yet they always send in some old ape, pathetically begging for attention. He doesn't know why these codgers insist on talking, as if their lives mean something to him. He never talks to them, yet wonders if they would consider giving him a quick tug. He would close his eyes.

He doesn't remember how long it's been since he touched a woman.  It may as well have been a hundred years. If he could only find a woman to lie down with, then the obsession could be pushed aside for awhile.  It's not that he wants a companion, he just wants to fuck. He's surprised that he uses the word fuck in his mind. He marvels at the certainty that fuck had never before passed his lips. He recognizes that fuck is a word used by a younger generation and using it would only cause problems.

dirk cowan

### Sextacular Spider-Man (Release Date: 2099)

Superheroes have been expanding beyond the comic book page into adult video stores and websites for years — *Invincible Iron Man on Man*, *XXX-Men*, to mention a few — and *Sextacular Spider-Man* is a welcomed entry, yet a problematic one.

Johnny Youngblood as *Peter Porker/Spider-Man* and Danni Deep as *Bonnie Joe Wantsom* ("Meet me in the abandoned factory, if you want your precious B.J!"), face off against the evil scientist Dr. Octopus played by Rex Topps. Youngblood, whose cock has been described more as a sprinkler than a sexual organ, is perfectly cast as the friendly-neighborhood superhero especially considering the sticky nature of spiders. Deep, the nubile and curvaceous newcomer has garnered accolades as an effortless star since debuting last month in *Big Wet Bottoms*, vol.18. Her performance as the plucky brain-washed, mind-controlled, and easily-seduced girlfriend however magnificent, gets lost amid the clumsiness of the film.

Nothing ruins a good spank-off like the fumbling of costumed porn stars. Scene after scene is filled with men grabbing and fucking blindly as their female leads hope to aim their co-star's cocks and thrusts. The best costume mishap and admittedly the most complex scene is the Doc Oct six-way, where rather than focusing on pleasuring his sex-minions, he spends the whole time making sure his fake appendages don't fall off. Luckily, the girls' impressive cock-skills help the fumbling Doc reach an unbelievable butakke-like climax, even if disappointingly his probing tentacles never find their way into their taut asses.

*Sextacular* is a spectacle, a high-wire fuck-fest, a film whose brim is overflowing with jizz — sorry, I mean webbing — and at times you can understand its filmmaker's vision, a blockbuster were hardcore sex is no longer the point but just another special effect ubiquitously filling each frame. Its problems aside, *Sextacular* should tingle any viewer's spider-sense.

ascot j. smith

### 1/3: A Busy Man

Bent knocked on Rad's door. He knew what he'd find when he got inside. Sure enough, Rad had been drinking wine and playing with himself. In the corner of the small room was a pile of crumpled tissues, into which Rad had spilled his seed. Bent smiled while Rad opened a bottle of wine. He held the cork in his hand and watched as Rad filled the glasses. Together they leaned against one of Rad's four walls, tilted their heads back, and let the wine crawl into their throats. It wasn't long before the first bottle was gone and both men were smiling. Rad reached for a second bottle and began to uncork it. Bent moved over to the corner of the room and, with the tip of a pencil, separated the crumpled tissues into piles of five. Eventually, there were six piles of five, and Bent said: "You've been a busy man, Rad." Rad nodded, smiled, and as he poured wine into the glasses, said: "Yes, Bent, that I have." With his toe, Bent pushed the tissues back into a single pile.

### 2/3: A Measuring

Bent and Rad stared at the walls for awhile and sipped quietly from their glasses. Bent tried to stand up straight, but fell back against the wall. "Your wine has made me heavy." he said to Rad, who had a grin on his mouth, but tears in his eyes. "My wine has made me sad." Rad said, and laughed while crying. Bent tossed his empty glass across the room. It landed, without breaking, on top of the pile of tissues. "You're lucky I've been so productive." Rad said. "Yes." Bent said, "But productivity never measures up to forty-seven minutes of pure tension." "True." Rad said, nodding his head. "But I only know my own little world of experience." When the second bottle of wine was gone, Rad produced a third. "This, then, is for splitting hairs." Bent said. "Yes," Rad said, "and when we have emptied it, you must measure it against the pile." He filled their glasses.

### 3/3: A Realization

Some time later, after the final bottle had been emptied, Bent closed his eyes and imagined that he had crawled into the bottom of a well, and that each time someone lowered a pail, he filled it with wine. Eventually, people came from everywhere to lower their pails into the well, until Bent

greg bachar

got bored and climbed up and out by opening his eyes. Meanwhile, Rad had closed his eyes and imagined that he climbed to the top of a tall tree in a park where lovers came at night to meet and hold each other in soft embraces. Every time a pair of lovers sat beneath his tree, Rad dropped a gold coin onto the grass next to them. Soon lovers came from everywhere to sit under the tree, until Rad ran out of coins and climbed down to the ground by opening his eyes. Rad looked at Bent, who held the empty bottle in his hand, and said: "Measure it." Bent threw the bottle across the room. It bounced off the pile of tissues and shattered against the wall. "Not good enough." Bent said. "No," said Rad, "Not good enough at all. There is much work to be done." "Well then," Bent said, "I'll let you get back to work. Thanks for the wine." Bent closed the door behind him and walked out into the street. Rad sighed. With a slight movement of his hand, he returned to work, after which he planned to take a very long nap.

you, come. grilled whorehouse steer. english toilet cuckold barbs. you come. junkie rigamarole. turning potentiality pierrot. four cherub lashings. scab, elbow and cheesecake bishop's sarcophagus. pesto chilblains with bowel tigress paste. mechanic ballcocks and nooses. parmesan-cuddled chimp. you: come. firefly-baked outbreak of cuckolded italian submariner meddlers and trollop placenta. spaceman cremation and childlike enchilada dipper. you. come. streetlight tosser pops. taste it. honeymoon perambulator-glazed chimera breeder saute and fur-rubbed peppermints. come taste. orchid and poppy seesaw calves. taste. come. melancholy lobes and whipped pouches. dutch appliance crumpet piggery. bonneted fried chloroform. titanic veiled payload handfuls. buttery oaf-squeezed rayon. taste it. come. you taste. goody-goody beached filmy diplomat. beggared paunches and grease. philistine-subculture steamroller and chevron panic. chemise and chiaroscuro blisters. indulgence and vendetta korma. its taste. hot poets handcuffed and chrysalis family value twister paddles. robotic reamed potentates, green beaters and rosemary buttonhole savagery. bandanna and smuggled cheerleader checkmate. taste you. spiky behest and bearskin burlap with rear choirboys. extravagant crony's easy fumbles. chump breeches, basement asphalt sauna and pasties. thin stomach nosebleeds with chromosomes. come taste. toffee screw in a poison satirist. pecker buyer cupping superintendent. backside yelp barbeque. come, taste. cognac crematorium piercing. taste, come. cretin chameleon and sideshow pardon. come, down.

joe milazzo

How can you be so cold afterwards? Twink said. And he laughed, and it was carried out over the trembling moon and into the trees.

Tomas didn't bother to roll over, didn't say a thing.

Twink moved onto his left hip, chin resting on Tomas' shoulder. Cum slid from foreskin to fleshy mud. The air smelled like sex and sulfur. Water slapped at the banks of the lake. It reminded him of the act, and that made his cock twitch and his balls roll around on his leg.

And he said, Ah, we fucked like bangtails, din't we? Then he leaned and whispered, Don't worry, babe. I'll still love ya tomorrow and tomorrow.

Tomas still didn't move.

Twink reached up for his jeans, gently brushing the bulky revolver into the mud, the barrel still warm to the touch. The roach-clip and lighter were in his front pocket.

You want a hit?

Tomas did not answer.

Twink shrugged and sat up. Then he cocked his head, lit the tiny speck and pursed his lips, kissing at the air. The red-hot cherry pulsed and then dropped, rolling across Tomas' bare thigh.

Oh! Sorry, Twink snorted, trying to hold it all in while brushing the ash from Tomas' thin, black leg hairs. Then his face reddened to purple, and he let it all spill out in a single, fabulous rush, and the smoke lost itself in the 3am mist.

c. m. connelly

i took Dove soap with me,
scrubbing dawn's doves into long
nights their wings beat feathers
into stinging fleshes of flight.

the muse is sick of the music
of her leaving, which was just, right,
too, now officer, she's not buried,
hear? among the poplars, cricks, & toads,

her *ohs* so sailing over the canopy
beneath which bullfrogs grunt ethereal
stories: long, moist, resonant, base:
the oncoming of a real stunner come.

again, the kind hers was just leaving, officer:
women in the night*mar* , tear named.
                    hair

steve halle

This salty cocoon of them seeding me nesting me teasing it out. Rubbing it over the pink over muffled cries. I could melt in that I could melt in that his delicious. Sexy wee fucker what I wouldn't give what I would give to have you here now jeeeeezus in the back of the car in the abandoned lot on marbled desk and so many hours spent beneath it. Tucked neatly. Convenient fucktoy small enough for a suitcase basket bottle. Nice legs salt and curve of her neck his neck    that space between front and back. Pink slap on her ass. A thumb. A finger.  I feel less alone when I.  Keeping the wife wet. Changing the sheets.  Wettly wettly. Flicking the tongue faster now head back his shower his ring. The fur of him the groan. The grasplessness the ache shudder regret and pleasure. The distance. Between his eyes. The green of them.  Uptilt of his brows. My sorrowful body. My giving of these little noises. Sound travels out. It is gifted.

To unburden myself of myself. To burden with him. With them. On every side every surface. Nest and bundle of them. The stroke the tug  face beneath the pillow. Grizzled furry ankled wrapped surrounded spread open slapped at tugged on abandoned muffled soaped up. Slippery legs pink warm and wet. The shower backseat the airport parking lot. The bourbon over her breasts champagne on his cock sheets in his ass     fec it the hob the jumper the lorry the bollard the abandoned castle still standing. The banter the tease. The first moments. Hours days weeks of wanting. Hunger. His knuckles. Their fingers. The rough of their hands. The leg up. The table. The right dirty. The bend and arch the grind the buckle the belt the swallow

kylee cook

My stepfather slept wherever he landed. Face down on the living room floor. His boxers inside out. Butt crack exposed. She was on the couch. Polishing her nails. Smacking gum like a freaken cow. Craig brought home his addiction. One of his addictions. Almost every night. They were all the same. This one wore lace panties and a top five times too small exposing her sagging melons that hung down to her waist. She spoke. Something about me making a pot of coffee. I ignored her and grabbed a can of Coke and a package of blueberry Pop Tarts. Five steps past my house and he pulls up. Josh. My on-again-off-again boyfriend. I never sit in the back seat of his car. On the torn vinyl seat open playboys almost reach the window. The floor is littered with stiff socks full of dried spunk. He admitted to me once that he reuses them. Josh stayed in the car when we arrived at school. He said he wanted to go over his trig answers. I knew better. He wanted to beat one off before first bell. Today I pass Jimmy and Toni. I think I saw her swallow. I never swallow Josh's. After school Josh and I ended up at the beach. He borrowed his friend's car. It was safe to climb into the back. We were in our undies. Steamed windows all around. Come on. He pleaded. I came close to letting his one-eyed wonder worm pop my cherry. But it belongs to me. My get out of jail card.

april gigliotti

Noah has memories of what it feels like to stand in water waist deep and look up at his big boat, this ark he is building, and think of how it was to be inside of a woman. Noah remembers the pairs of legs like animals walking up the plank and how they will moan and beg when he has finished the deck he is building, when he moves from the curved flanks to the smoothed deck to the walls and the ceiling of this memory, taking her clothes off from bottom to top, building a revelation.

When Noah was holding a woman it was like holding this enormous ship up on his arms, like cuddling her lips and bending her down and towards himself. There was a woman for every freckle on his body and a sigh for every nail he had pounded in. The bomb-rain that had come down before the actual rain started coming down before Noah was this Noah building this ark watching this world go under water, before then him holding a woman in his arms and weeping his own kind of inglorious muted rain.

Half-built is a half-woman who holds Noah above his memories and drops him down like into water. Noah has boards and nails and a hammer and arms made of saw-blades. The women in his memory have collaged into one woman with the head of an antelope and the thighs of a horse and the torso of a gorilla and the chest of a rhinoceros. And all the other animals are involved, all and each taking a piece of the memory of the women that he has, rolled into one woman, seeping atop once-dry sheets, waving on these waves with Noah, his ark as always only half—ever-finished.

j. a. tyler

Dove's eyes washed with milk. I chew them slowly. His left hand whispers. Comfort me with apples and the empty space around them. Drops of the night slide down a thread of scarlet. His pillars of smoke have covered me in the good all-day-long smell. I seek the honey under your tongue. A wedge of pomegranate lodged in a socket of gold. I nibble the folds of old leather underarms. Putrid gelatin seeps from his sagging pucker. Bursts of cunning mountain spices push me to the desolate edge. Enclosed in boards of cedar. Nostrils snaking spikenard and myrrh. The dangling image atrophies. The mirror sends you back. Sifting through my papers. Stealing through your hours. Shitting on a shingle. His right hand takes all the time. In my swimming holes he wets himself to fertilize delirium. Jack in the box you mother fuck. The midst is paved with your glove. Make me feel animal. More wetness on my toes. Calamus knights in masquerade or gadgets in arrears? We upturn stones to watch the worms writhe in sudden light. And sketch rare birds on un-mopped floors. Number two. Pencil clenched in teeth. A flabbergasted mannequin begs me. Stop. Not until the mandrakes bleed. Not until your thoughts are smeared. Auburn leaves of autumn scratch spells on hidden flesh. White letters on waxed paper. Infinity coils. Hot coals of my joy take refuge in all objects as they enter. Lilies that fester in a blistering clitch. This soft goblet once craved brutal ointments. My skin came away wrinkling in both his hands. And now his cavaliering stance hangs charmed and silver. Tender grapes cluster against the lattice. I sear each word he speaks with my cigarette.

rob stephenson

Your flesh considers mine
    Your voice but

I am to be committed
your voice is a song
your voice is music

I've been the cause of desire the source of desire
the waves they will never cease
I would ask you to cleave me in two
I would be something more
I would be rising energy          a piercing
but moon is
I would hesitate with my lips, fingers, breast  on your
      because my blood
shivering skin      tickle of hair      heat
we would be flesh to flesh
our blood rushes to the lips to the breast to the thighs to the labia the shaft
    we would be filled
be warmth and fluid
Say you don't want to go here
Say taboo
The one who spreads apart your two thighs
Say a pushing away
Who licks the inside of your womb
There is a fury in the touch      I am the source and the cause
I am the desire
I want

jennifer calkins

your flesh

There's a fire under the earth
There's a fire
A stream                              our souls
                    These are just bodies
                    These are just lips and tongue and teeth
                    These are just nails raking backs
                    These are just your lips on my breasts
                    This is just my hand on your ass
This is just your cock approaching, touching, entering, pushing into this is just fluid and you inside
of me
                    Just
He fumbles                                                        at your
Soul
He fumbles
He spreads
          Raking          Shuddering
Was a shuddering
spreads apart your two thighs
                    He touched me
I live to know          licks the inside
Spreads apart          shuddering in the essence
Shuddering
It is good, it is lifting
It is good here it is good
It is lifting
it is good I have been lifted
I am lifted          good
I am

*Some portions of this text were appropriated from*
*Emily Dickinson, Nicole Brossard, The Rig Veda,*
*Isabelle Eberhardt, Ingeborg Bachman*

She loved the nausea. Loved the weight she lost from it. Kept getting pregnant just to feel it. Then, once the first trimester was over she'd abort and rest for a bit before starting the process over again. She'd find clean, random men who loved unsafe sex. Then she'd take her leaky prize home to her lover; the lover she loved; who liked her starved and skinny.

She stumbled upon this trick by accident. All steps from conception to illness to death were acts of chance. But ever after she conducted the orchestra of birth sickness and loss. The cycle of life devoured one after another inside her for no other reason than the ecstatic thrill and power. A power greater than what all those second rate anorexics had in mind. She applied science to her psychosis and so, perfected it.

Her lover never knew. Or at least did not act like she knew. Didn't care about the method either way. Just results. And the results were good. Of course she realized there were men. But men did not matter to her. They were just dildos with cardiovascular systems. The only downside was the disease that those beasts carried, but all things have a downside. At least she found clean specimens; was careful in her reckless ways.

How she kept having periods at all was the real mystery, but she figured if those organs were the ones that wanted to work then they'd be exploited for her benefit. She wondered once how the children would have looked, if she ever bothered to see a single one to term. Then she thought of the men she had been with and felt better.

theresa o'donnell

Buddha Was A Deadbeat Dad: *George Bailey and Vy Bick revisited in Bedford Falls, ten years later...*

Vy pulled her gown off over the top of her head. No sooner had he crawled in on top of her than something wonderful began to happen: her smile widened and she seemed to melt, almost becoming a liquid while George began his ponderous movement over her. When they made love, George wished he had married Vy... He kissed her mouth passionately and held her breast in one hand as he sawed back and forth, rousing Vy to new levels of excitement.

She was so sensual, the most sensual woman he had ever known. Vy moaned softly and closed her eyes, coiling her legs around his waist and cinching her heels as she clung tightly to him.

"I'm going to stuff you GOOD, Vy," George snarled. "You no-good, filthy, cyprian!" He wasn't mad at Vy; it was a little game they played. It excited Vy when George talked dirty to her.

"You know what I'm gonna do to you, nob-gobbler?"

She began to hiss like a steam valve. "I'm going to take this meat-machine and drive it to Jutland!" Violet's breasts shook violently and now Georgie-boy was getting excited too as she began to breathe heavily, "Uh-ah-ah-uh, OH-OH-OH!"

"You know what I'm gonna do then, Vy? I'm going to make you lick that mud-stained jackhammer!"

Vy's eyes shot wide, lost their focus and rolled up to the top of her head as a grand mal seizure overwhelmed and split her, mouth-opened, an agonized yodel that wild dogs might have envied pealing from her lips and throat. George watched in amazement as Violet started to come, then let himself go. Floating in their carnal wreckage, they found each other's mouths and lips like blind moles.

"Vy, Vy, I love you, Violet Bick."

dennis weiser

I wheel the rim of the rocky trail, circling, circling, furiously circling the head until I can tease myself no more. I plunge in, tires disappearing in thick clouds of dust.

To the other BMX-ers, I am known as the poet bunny in a skirt. They pack together, boys showing off their Ramrodders and the drillium to their frames, closing me out. E.E. Cummings and I, though, are not the usual bunny hop.

I take to the air, launching over the crest of a hill, suspended a moment with the snaps of my skirt ends fanning behind me, a guttural grunt swallowing the first rough landing. E.E. shudders and begs beneath for me to take in so much more. I'm careful, though, not to devour the entire enormous rubber shaft so early in the ride, instead just pogo-ing the plump, moist noggin.

Handling the wooded path, I yell E.E.'s poetry: "All in green my love went riding,"—sinking my knees a little more to where the seat should be, the bulging cock push-pushing deeper—"On a great horse of gold."

I save "I Like my Body when it is With Yours" for stump grinding. Furthest, in the abyss of bush-darkened trail, the dick punches hard with each grind of the succession of tree stumps. "I like/ slowly stroking the," I ride E.E.'s jolting, driving, sheer intoxication. "Shocking fuzz of your electric fur"—boing-boinging over more stumps. "And what-is-it," the sweat pops out of my pores now, every hair follicle on end—"comes over parting flesh." E.E. corkscrews me into the air, sailing and trembling, awaiting that final landing. And when it comes, finally, we collapse together in a groundswell of poetry and sweat and earth and sheer afterglow.

rion woolf

Big Barb's boobs bobbled in the moonlit like two giant tubs of quivering jello. She never really achieved an ecstatic climax, but ever few minutes her two hundred and fifty pound body tensed and she let out a deep kinda animal growl. This went on and on as the boys took turns fucking her. On her back on a blanket in a wooded glade beside a corn field on a hot August Iowa night, a beer in her left hand and a fist full of rubbers in the other, she methodically went about her pleasure. With Barb you could always find the wet spot without rolling her in flour. After each boy finished she shout out "who wants some more!" Big Barb, with gusto, pulled that long, long train—choo choo, choo choo ch'boggie.

Rarely, did anybody volunteer for seconds, except one guy who went back several times. He musta had a dick the size of a baseball bat or he tied a board on his ass to keep from falling in, but Barb loved him. Half drunk she muttered, "I'm taking this son-of-bitch home with me." And, when her husband was out-of-town, she did.

Throughout the extravaganza the bangers hung around the car, all four doors open, listening to the radio, sitting on the hood and leaning against the fence post with a beer can clutched in their fists. Nobody said much of anything either before or after. Occasional eye contact was inevitable, but avoided, as it revealed a questioning sense of shame. What in the fuck were we doing banging a fat lady in a hay field? Ironically, the Bud song wafted quietly from the car radio as background music for the bacchanalia:

When you say "Bud"
You've gone as far as you can go to get the very best
When you say "Bud"
You've said the word that means you like to do it all
When you say "Bud"

hal wert

Tad's stomach slightly churned as he thought, "Yep, what the fuck, I guess we're doin' it all." Tad cracked another beer, a Grain Belt, as he witnessed three of the boy's reach out their hands and help pull Barb up on to her feet. The blanket was covered with smashed empty beer cans and used rubbers. Wobbly, she yanked a sheet from a roll of paper towels, wiped out her cunt, and hiked up her huge J.C. Penney's pink panties. With a triumphant "fuck you" look on her face, she waddled to the car. On the trip back to town nobody said a thing. Dropping Barb off in front of her favorite tavern the boys chorused, "Good night Barb, thank you. We'll see you again." Barb didn't look back as her two huge arms pushed open the double glass tavern doors. Occasionally home from college, Tad heard whispers that that hay field train to nowhere was still running--Choo choo, choo choo, ch'boggie.

When this woman told me she'd been on the rack, she got me all cranked up. "I went to this sex retreat," she said. "They had this table that turned into a rack."

I had this picture of a table with rollers and winches, and gears and cinches. "Tell me more," I begged.

"When they stretched me, my waist got narrower. The more they pulled, the narrower it got. It got so narrow you could put your fingers around it."

I thought about wasp waists, seen only on wasps and women on the rack. Well, maybe a corseted waist could come close to a wasp waist. But I was more medieval than Victorian. I wanted to get hold of the heavy equipment. I wanted to put on a pointy black hood and turn the wheel. "Is there a place where we can find a starter rack?" I asked. "Are there racks for home use?"

"I have a bag of toys," she said, "but I don't have a torture table."

The toys were fine, I thought. I could maybe find a pointy hood among them. But I needed a platform for stretching, a Procrustean bed. I wanted to shape her waist into that of a wasp—a thread between the thorax and abdomen. Then I wanted to put my fingers around it. But I didn't want to stop with the waist. I wanted to move to the breasts. I want to see them start as melons, then become mangoes, then pancakes with with blueberries in the middle. Yes, I was ready to turn the wheel at breakfast—and lunch and dinner.

When everything was extended, I would bring out my knife, fork and tongs. You can't rack someone without using your tongs. I would throw the brassiere into the charcoal brazier, then I would heat up the pincers. With the hood and the tongs, I would rack to the max. I'd be the boss of my own racket. I'd be a sex racketeer.

thaddeus rutkowski

My tongue desired mud, longed to remember the innocence of a quiet mirror. The roots of her words inside my mouth mixed with saliva. Forgotten moments of nameless fingers, fists, and unspeakable objects.

Another old man in some alley, stinking of polyester, holding a twenty. Come hither. Shards of glass still stuck in my boyish tender knees from last night and the night before that and the night before that and. My throat raw. My lips blistered. "Do you know what happens to me on the inside when you put your finger there on the outside?" My body a funny Valentine for blind men with calloused hands. "Can I be your girl? If it be your will?" He ignored me and with every movement of his lonely muscles he cracked my little girl dreams in half. He used his hands to choke me, to teach me about silence, about obedience.

Years later I stand at the river with Jo. She says when I dream I am always a man and I crack your ribs open to penetrate you, to get to the inside, to return to the beginning. With each touch she erases words from my skin and with one little boy kiss I become her girl. Her blood, her breath, enter me. We leave fingerprints all over each other.

And in the morning our skin, our words, are covered in dark river mud. The filth of lost memories.

doug rice

Margins
By Alyssa Wisener

I AM BI.
4 out of 5
Gays Lesbians Straights
agree:

I DON'T EXIST
for there are but 2 orientations:
gay OR straight.

MY TRUE IDENTITY:
a girl seeking bros seeking 3sums
a lesbian unwilling to forsake hetero-privilege

IRRELEVANT
that I have fucked guys and girls
cum from cocks while tonguing cunts

i don't exist.

I AM SWITCH.
9 out of 10
Dom/mes subs painsluts or sadists
agree:

I DON'T EXIST

alyssa wisener

for there are but 3 orientations:
Dom/me OR sub OR vanilla

MY TRUE IDENTITY:
a Domme who needs practice
a sub who cannot accept her rightful place
a vanilla who is trying to seem interesting.

IRRELEVANT
that I have Dommed AND submitted
attained headspace AND subspace
enjoy receiving pain AND causing marks
that I am neither Top nor bottom
but a person capable of flying AND crawling.

I EXIST.


Balanced on the border
between straight and gay
between Dom/me and sub
between being and not-being
is a bisexual switch.

My magic is in my tension,
my need to play on the edge,
my need to BE the edge

SELF / nothing
I am the slash.

I'm no skinflint, but I like skin. It doesn't have to be smooth skin; it can be bumpy skin. It can be chicken skin, but not on a chicken. No, I'm talking about human skin. Not flesh, either. Or meat, though I have nothing against flesh or meat, as long as they are not on the table. Unless I am doing something on the table, something like forking, if forking is what I have to do.

What is a skinflint anyway? Is that a flinty sort of guy, a guy with a piece or two of flint, ready to strike a spark and burn some skin? I have to say, I do not like my skin burnt, by the sun or any other means. I mean, why not keep the flesh fresh?

I'm talking about hide. There's something about hide that draws me like a fly. I'm hidebound in my fixation with hide. I'm bound to bind hide; I was born to do it. I'm not talking about cowhide; I mean people hide, the kind you can't hide. When I see that kind of hide, I say, "Hi de ho," and then I go in for some skin.

I know the idea is you gotta tear off a piece. I've heard it many times: "If you want to be a man, you've got to rip off a piece." But I like my skin intact, all in one piece. I might tickle it, slap it, pin it, strap it, or whip it. But I'm not going to shred it. I'll save shredding for legal documents, papers that prove I'm a skinflint. Those go into the chipper.

thaddeus rutkowski

Stacey always says that the month before her first period, when she was fourteen, she laid an egg. She says it was the size of a chicken egg but the shell was purple—like a vein—she always says—like a big, pulsating vein. She says its shell was soft when she laid it and covered in thick mucus. Says she pulled it out of the toilet, rinsed it off and saved it for about a week, but that it began to smell foul so she had to throw it out. She says she tried to keep it warm. Hid it under her pillow, and sat with it between her thighs, trying to hatch it.

Says she was real sad when she had to throw it out. Says it never happened again. Stacey isn't a liar, but she must be lying about this. She says she never uses tampons in case she might lay another one. But that doesn't explain why she refuses to use pads. We all have sick habits.

She can't have babies. One of her ovaries is missing. Was never there. That's what she says.

 Stacey eats yolk-drenched French toast every Sunday at Denny's and tells me about her husband, and her mistress, and her pet rat. She always drips syrup on her shirt. Sometimes it rolls down her chest and sticks to her breasts. She laughs it off.

She thinks she was an ostrich in a past life. She tells me I used to be a toad. I just want to wash her blood off my couch and wonder what she will become in her next incarnation.

theresa o'donnell

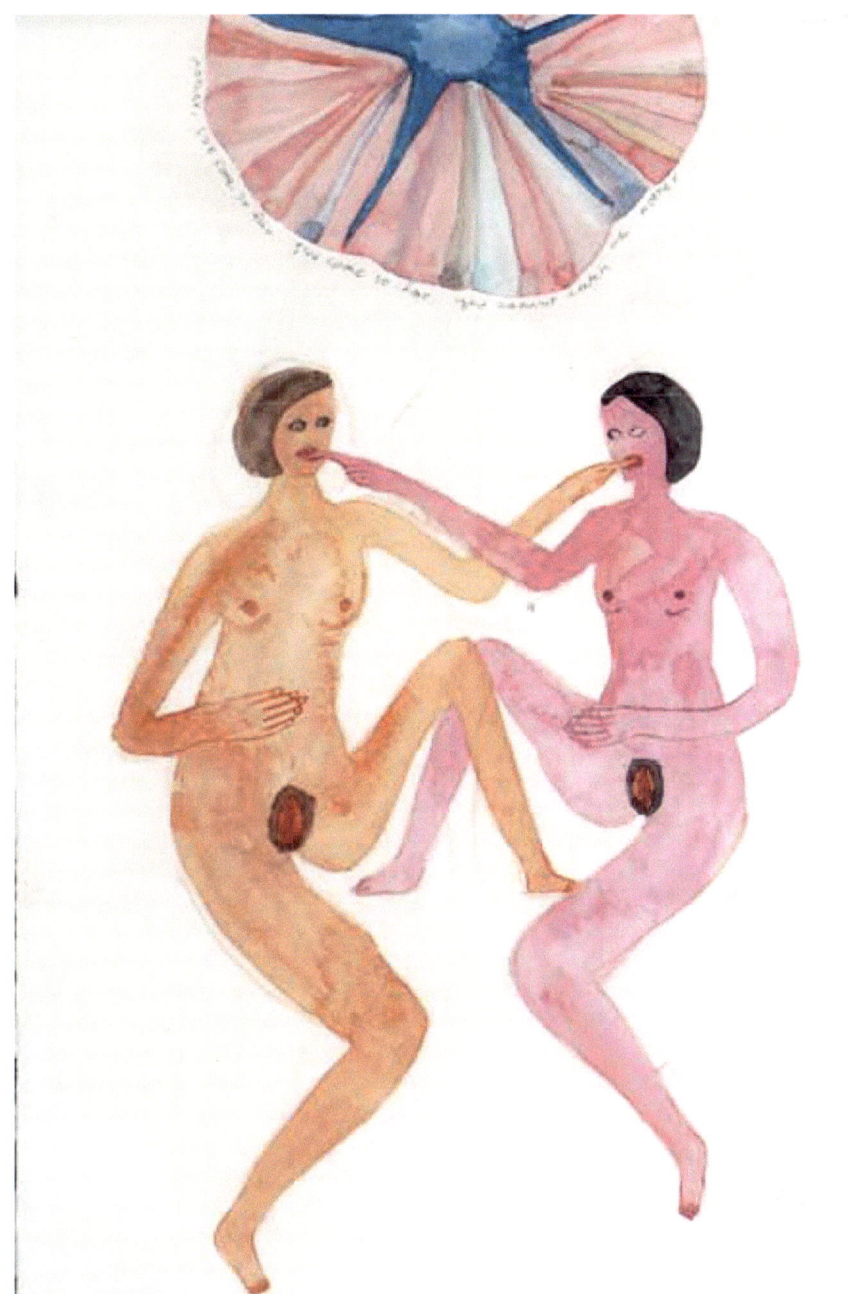

His gate is that of an elephant, lumbering, methodical, two hours from sober. She waits, a flightless bird heavy with plumage, neck craned, her quandary: bury her head and allow the encroachment, or dart for the open range. His once flaccid trunk has stiffened, protruding as his anticipation builds, infusing his approach with primal energy, the impossible geometry of a giraffe in full lope, panting, stopped short by her insistence.

She pulls her head from the sand, eying the savannah, calculating the steps, the speed at which she would have to dart, a gazelle, perhaps. He senses the prey, stalking her, a tiger on the scent of a fresh kill, driven by instinct, by experience, and the promising mixture of department store perfume and vodka, a scent he know will lead to the prize.

She eases down, her shoulder blades pinned back, waiting in butterfly position. The ravenous tiger has lost all ferocity watching his prey acquiesce. She is comfortable and unthreatened, not the least bit intimidated by the size of his teeth. Then finesse, it must be, aptitude in lieu of raw power, a fox eying the rabbit hole.

He suddenly penetrates the rabbit hole, working his head into the opening, just enough, at first, before pulling out. The walls of earth are warm as he works in his entire body, lower this time, driving for the bundle of fur, passive, huddled in the corner. In and back out, pushing on the walls of the hole, further each time, working so hard to reach the rabbit. His stamina falters. He sees the rabbit. She turns around. Her fur wet, teeth exposed. The fox finds not a rabbit, but the firm jaw of a badger that consumes him.

m. e. parker

Therefore, she began with a cliché.

"Fuck you Bradley Bench."

The last words Lorraine Bristol spoke to him. The last because she died (aw geez – died? for real?) three months after st-st-st-stuttering herself out of their relationship. She only st-st-st-stuttered when she was horny. Or so she s-s-s-s-said when he questioned her four minutes after he stabbed his hand with his salad fork, three minutes before he read her palm.

"N-not all the t-t-t-t-time," she replied.

During their six-month relationship, however, he discovered the only times he heard her stutter-free were after he fucked her throat. After the first time he felt his cum slip past her uvula, he retracted his dick and asked her for the time.

"A quarter to six," she said, clearly articulating each phoneme. "What's for dinner?"

Hearing her without her stutter unnerved him – like seeing someone's puckered bald head without their wig or someone's dry eye socket when their glass eye popped out. He had come to depend upon her stutter, as much as he depended on the russet stains that marked her side of the bed or the way her nostrils dilated when she came. As much as he enjoyed sticking his hard dick in her warm, wet mouth, his subconscious yearning for her stutter soon manifested itself physically – at first he couldn't cum, but it wasn't long until his dick stayed soft.

It's why they broke up. He stopped having sex with her and instead started up with a blow-up doll named Irene. He could fuck Irene's throat all he wanted, without any worries that she would lose her stutter. She would be the perfect woman if not for the fact that she knew she was perfect. And, Bradley rationalized, anyone who thinks they're perfect can't be.

kathleen miller

## Dearest love, my beauty

as a garment, you are white;
as a season, you are spring;
as a flower, you are jasmine;
as a perfume, musk;
as a beauty; pure modesty; and
as a being, you are love;
to you and none other
I address this letter.

Indulge me. Grant me one (of many) wishes.
Go back and read the beginning of this
letter out loud, to yourself. Open your
heart. Be calmed and allow my love to fill
your every hollow and void even as my prick
grows to fill your expanding cunt and we
exchange juice; even as I explore the folds
of your womanness, your bounteous love.

Take my words to heart as you draw me to
your breast. Read and re-read them until
lubrication drips from the opening I long
to kiss, to lick, to suck, to taste in all
its sweetness.

Re-read my testament to you until
you may form it into a tool the precise
dimension of my erect penis. Insert it.
Move it outside, in and out gently
out and around and over again recite my
words as a litany.

Rocking knees, arched back, thrust the
shaft formed of my words, shaped
by your intention. Face buried, ass raised,
again imagine again my penetration.

Do whatever is required and don't be
miserly with the juice of your climax.
Spray my cheeks, soak a pillow. Indulge me
so that at our next meeting even our talk
of weather is about love and in just our
teasing play we might exchange s[k]ins.

j. m. rees

animation stuck my          thighs between the tips touched
enable the length      of these arms to     touch     to screen the
youth –       O youth     a determinism        to
touch      your hand     against        hand against my
against my       – almost
     where I'd never want     yr hands
          tip to face     allocate spaces     leopards in
between     lion's den palate               – upper        and all
teeth
   how to bleed       O please bleed and turn
        a bit for me                    or a spit on yr
stake       rival the costumed dead
     O touch for me     O creep for me
in yellowed narcissus   in late spring       stranger faced and
open          for business                    open to crack
yr teeth   or              my skull          almost
almost          there     the   leatherback eats     yr
 principle skin

kimberly koga

He typed; she anxiously bit her lower lip.

There were alterations to the typewriter, how its mechanisms were arranged and moved. He had rigged it this way, and she had not anticipated this. With each key pressed, each harsh snap of impact against paper, the platen turned. The long cylinder was rolling continuously as his fingers worked across the keys.

F-R-O-W-N-A-L-L-Y-O-U-W-A-N-T-I-T-W-I-L-L-S-T-I-L-L-K-E-E-P-T-U-R-N-I-N-G-

And as it spun, it pulled and wound the thin, blue thread further onto itself. This lifeline of material fed from the base of her tight sweater, unwinding in one inexorable draw. The lowest portion of it had already risen quite high, disappearing as the typewriter consumed it. She knew he could see concern in her bare stomach, how it moved as she breathed. He was watching her there.

She pleaded; he admonished, transcribing their conversation word-for-word.

P-L-E-A-S-E-

Her small stool creaked as she began another incremental rotation, furthering the unwind. Already, the lower rim of her full breasts started to show below the rising fabric line. His hand strayed close to the carriage return lever and she winced, pressed her eyes tight together. If the carriage jerked to the side, it ultimately pulled two thin jewelry chains, which pulled the rings set into her nipples, If he would just depress the carriage release, however, their session would end.

She sought an economy of words, feverishly seeking to say less and conserve thread, yet negotiate for release. Words were considered, rejected, discarded. New ones played near the end of her tongue.

N-N-N-

When she realized he was transcribing her moans and non-words on the typewriter, she felt dizzy. He paused, tips of fingers barely contacting the smooth plastic of keys. Lips moved, but wouldn't breathe words. One drop of sweat rolled down across skin.

R-E-L-E-A-S-E-

eric jeitner

This is how you know she's a bitch: ieeee!!!!! This is how you know he's a dick: grrrrrr. This is the Bean Blaster 5000: don't put it on the highest setting right away, or it will blast your bean off. This is the laundry detergent: pour liquid up to the third line for a full load. This is the Lotus For Men: putting lubrication inside the toy might be more comfortable, but it is difficult to clean because of the suction cups. This is the broken beam in the father's garage. This is the sticky mouth: time to wash it out. This is that phone number. This is the adult toy cleaner: spray on for fifteen seconds, allowing the solution to penetrate the crevices of the toy, then wipe off with a clean towel. This is the man who tried to get off by hanging himself in his father's garage. This is the blue lubrication that stings when you put it on your clit or the tip of the penis, right on the part where it comes together like the top of a construction paper cut-out heart. This is the blindfold scarf. This is the woman who hits: see her eyes? This is the book we are a little ashamed of. This is the pretty spot. This is the pill. This is that drink that is pricy. This is the bruise from when he fell when the beam broke. This is the dirty sheet in the hamper. This is the silk bag that the lubrication comes in: it is expensive. This is the rope that he tried out: it was used for the tire swing when he was little.

melanie page

It was autumn, so we slung her over the split-rails to dry in the crisper breezes, knowing the smoky air – there, near the now brittle briers we'd set ablaze – would trap the piquant flavor of her and keep it that way all through the winter. The sweet meat where there were once tight curls of flaming red hairs... the lips bare now; smooth and coolly slender. The throbbing over; the tender folds liberally salted, the blood carefully drained. In spring, she was succulent to the eye – engorged, even, to the point where she'd driven us mad! We'd warned her: "From here, we can see your thigh!" She'd laughed, though – her mirth like tinkling bells strung through plum blossoms that are caught on the gentle wind of an April rain. We could hardly fault her for it – that blithe laugh. She'd seemed as intoxicated by spring as the dewy hyacinth blossoms, or as the swollen buds of the old roses that had not yet burst with their sultry fragrance of sin. She'd refused to believe us, yet here was her proof: gone now, from the waist up. Splitter-splatter went the shards of bone in blood. "Straighten your skirts," we'd urged her; "don't sit that way – we're going balmy!" Lewdly was how she sat, legs splayed down in the grass, those flowery dresses with their many underskirts of lace raised too high. Until it was plain that she'd worn nothing under those lacy skirts, that the fleshy folds beneath the tight red curls were swollen and dripping something salty-sweet. In the summer, she was even worse. ("I want to devour you," I'd whispered once, my fingers plunging into her while I lost control of my very breath. I licked them then – my fingers – and madly kissed the side of her dampening face.)

marilyn jaye lewis

# Two Yoo-Hoos

Two yoo-hoos hung:
the moon is if music
reads red into early.
havest what is left
of what holds?
color, flavonoid, eclipse:
a garnish on nothing.　o
& as she comes　　　　blood-
into her own void　　　　　　shit
eyeshot　　　　　　　　moon
a bent note.　　　　o-
　　　　　　　　ver

steve halle

I cannot always manage to live up to my past. Now and again I see a chance to better it, to put her in my shadow for a change. Oh she didn't like to. Well I love nothing more, even if I don't and it hurts and is like no discomfort I have ever known. Being her is not of prime importance all the time, it seems. Never have I sat astride the pale trembling flesh of some lean young buck half my age, tempering his rigid mayhem with the composure of an old school mistress. Am I to believe only ever him? Never have I licked the sweat from a soldier's armpits as he pinned my arms to the ground and fucked me guileless, his brass rivets chaffing my inner thigh. A spit-roast is off the menu for lovers like us. When he puts his head between my legs just who I am is an irrelevance – as long as I am connected to my clitoris in the ways that matter. He slurps and sucks like an aardvark with its snout in a termite mound, and I discourage his head from dislodging itself by clamping my hands to his scalp. I close my eyes and it's as black as bad blood, black as lung shadows, black as the deepest fathom, black as a little dress, black as Susan's eyes, black as bitumenized gloom, black as darkling sable... I bring my tits up to my mouth and smother them in my tart's lipstick, and it's like my areolae are spreading across my breasts. How I wiggle and squirm as he does his work on me: a worm on a hotplate. But then it's over in a crescendo of spasms and expletives, and I return to forget.

gary j. shipley

I remind him of his first Rebecca, the woman who taught him what love was. I'm in another world, and he's making love to me like I'm a woman, telling me more of the things he has done to Rebecca.

"I love you," he says.

Fuck my face, Rebecca said to Richard. I want you to fuck my face.

No, he said. I want you to fuck my face. I want you to ride my face.

This isn't going to work, she said. I don't want your tongue in my pussy any more than I want it in my mouth.

Maybe I'm not as good as Rebecca. She never knew what submission was. That's why he wanted her.

After getting dressed, we go back to Richard's apartment, again, where he shows me how he wants the dream women arranged in his bedroom, how he wants the imaginary Rebecca positioned before his giant mirrors.

Removing my clothes, he turns me upside down and into the imaginary Rebecca by bending me so that my ass is high in the air like in the photo.

"Rebecca," Richard says. "Oh, my sweet."

He rides me like a demon on a bike.

Afterwards, I'm so tired I sleep without dreaming, waking when he takes my face in his hands, smears transparent pink gloss on my lips, and kisses me like a lover would.

aimee parkison

We both pretend his dick is as hard as a rock. Even while he's obsessively masturbating like a patient in a mental hospital, his limp dick resembles a dead shell-less turtle with a broken neck. He asks me to lick his asshole while attempting to bring the dead turtle back to life. I spend night after night pretending the turtle isn't dead, that the turtle hasn't been dead for months. That's how I know I still love him, even when he whispers a stranger's name in sleep and for a moment the turtle looks like it might revive itself.

Our language is born of silence. It comes from the eyes of women and girls, as they stare at themselves in mirrors, long after we have given up trying to translate what their words might really mean. The language flows into the eyes of a man like me who sees himself in Richard's mirrors and does not recognize himself as a man, because he does not long to possess women but to become them. I dream of mastering men's turtles, of holding them, possessing them, bringing dead turtles back to life. For the next three hours, Richard masturbates intermittently, an interior-design magazine and trench coat on his lap while he tells me exactly how he will fuck me. The magazine keeps falling off the trench coat, which moves crazily like a cat trapped beneath fabric. Richard keeps running out of breath. I just sit on my bed, hands folded, listening in a quiet yet professional manner. Staring at pornographic photos, he says, "The lesbians will obey my every command." The turtle is still dead. Not even our imaginary lesbians can bring it back to life.

aimee parkison

I show him photos of three sex workers from Madrid. The beauty of it all is they know each other. They actually enjoy each other's company, so they won't be fucking for him, or for me. They'll be fucking for themselves. On the back of one of the photos, I read the inscription – Take me . . . by surprise. "Chameleon, Phoenix, and Lynx," I say, holding up the three images. Chameleon, the brunette with green-brown eyes, lies spread-eagle over scratched hardwoods, her eyes staring into the camera. She has lovely eyes, dramatically arched brows, and pretty pale smooth feet with pointed toes like a dancer. She's smooth and toned, her long dark hair like silk. Phoenix, the redhead, is captured in a sunlit pool of brilliant blue water, her bright hair floating weightlessly around arms and breasts and belly. Her nipples are pink, sparkling in the sun. She's pouting at the camera like the child she is, her brilliant eyes matching the blue water, slender fingers splayed beneath tiny breasts. The blond Lynx is the final image, an exquisite woman on all fours, her rump high in the air and pointed at the camera so that anyone can stare into her asshole and her eyes at the same time. The silken refinement, waves of glistening stands flow across face and body as she turns, sweeping from feet to legs to chest to groin to belly to chest, and then to what I fear is the true nakedness – my expression. Masturbating constantly, a man might come beneath the shadow of her hair so she could mop up the semen with luxurious strands. The blond and the redhead watch – waiting, approving – no words, no sound but breath.

aimee parkison

Sometimes Kami liked to love gently. To play. Would put food behind her knees, sit on a chair, back facing Martha, and ask her to taste. Honey, cream cheese, mustard, soy sauce. Always a surprise. Martha's lips would curl under her teeth and lick them.

"You are a delicious tease."

"Quiet, darling. Try the other side."

Sometimes Kami wanted to be hit hard in the ribs with the splintered bat that Martha had been fucking her with.

"Come on, baby, stop pumping, start swinging. I want something new to bleed."

"Shut up, you liquid dyke. You wood whore. I'm gonna go after your ass next. Treat you like a boy fag. You want that? How about that instead of rib splitting? I'll give you a hate crime. Is that what you want? You slut. You know a hate crime will make you cum all over your battering ram."

Sometimes they'd dress up like animals and pretend to be different crimes of nature. "Meooowwwww!"

"BaaaaAAA, Uhhhh."

And sometimes things were just quiet. No games, no costumes. Just hands and tongues. Clutching. Squeezing. Holding. Dripping. Mouths too full to say a word.

theresa o'donnell

Halfway through the building of his ark Noah sees a light-feathered bird pouring through the rain and for the moment of a raindrop falling from a cloud remembers how it used to look when a woman stepped over towards a bed and how he would lay his head back and close his eyes and imagine a world that eternally soft and liquid. And halfway through this moment of a raindrop dropping from the sky Noah remembers that the ark is only half built and that he needs to pound by himself for as long as it takes given this saw and this hammer and these nails and his muscled lonely hands, to build this to float what remains.

Noah was a man on a bed waiting for a woman in the doorway who was waiting for the next strike of lightning the next bout of thunder before she removed the black garters from her legs before she unlaced the corset from her back before she set down upon Noah like two animals side by side on an ark already rolling seas. It doesn't take a bird for Noah to remember this woman. It only takes the pivot of lightning above and the crush of rain, the settling of wet down his legs again to sticky up the mess, to bring down the nails through the wood and onward in his building he goes.

If Noah pauses for too long the rain and the thunder and the lightning they will swallow him up. He remembers a woman and he remembers her mouth. He remembers what it means to swallow. He remembers how it was to feel full after a meal at a dining room table where the ceiling above his head wasn't missiled open. He remembers rain when it wasn't raining bombs and it wasn't a flood. He remembers being dry and then being wet, of a sudden pulsing moment, the large trickery between men and women, the breaking open of gates where behind is all the water in the world and all the water over it, until the bough breaks.

j. a. tyler

Failed future fetuses rained like lightly mixed plaster of Paris upon the face of angels. Putting on their cherubic birthday suits, obediently kneeling and on their best behaviour. Tails wagged were there any, and there were plenty.

Cocks and cunts in a cocktail mix. Warm brown volcanoes where nymph eats nymph.

I felt dirty, like I wanted to be.

I lapped at wet musky fingers that smell of my sex. That brings memories of my ex, of her serpentine coil around my lust, and her epic bouncy bust.

...And the tone of her moans, and the shape of her mons, and the taste, oh sweet Jesus, the taste! Oh SWEET LORD!!!

The computer screen spluttered, and my Freudian atrophied cock coughed its first, of what would be many more, on this first night alone.

nabila najwa

I text with my ying-yang. Aniset keeps this Johnson hard but her pussy no longer accessible. We reek together. Lesions pus out from collar and cuffs.

We nastied in the stockyards once. Huge drops of rain dropped. Rolled in slopshit of beasts that are hustled away to make burger meat. "I am turned on by scars!" She scores my cheek with a rusty nail. Blood, whoa! rgsm sns vwls. Sweet Garlips the child sprang from those greasy moments. Looks like turd sausages, breath like the farts of a bulldog licking scuzz off a fast food dumpster. It's a tattoo dog, licks blood and ink. Do you tattoo?

Aniset texts with erect nipple; I text with my schlong. Smell it, dude. I am the top misogynist of the whole world so eat my shit. On Winky, the home planet, we are all creeps, proud creeps. She too does joyously misogynize. It's a standoff.

Wormhole is a pungent tunnel of scooch through which we slithered. Soft and nasty pulses in the squeeze around you as you go. For me it was AWITP Now my peckertweets flash to your belly. Above the navel, yes. Below, no!

The only tattoo I portaled with me is on my dick. When Aniset moves Fort Bushie near we can read the tats along my hard beef bayonet. Rules of the game -- NEVER PUT THE WISHBONE WHERE THE BACKBONE OUGHT TO BE, MIND THE GAP, DON'T LOOK BACK, STAY IN LINE etc.. Turkey neck into cooze, we lose. It's like Helen of Troy, boy.

Sweet Garlips smells like shit. Makes us proud. Aniset drops under the table, turns loose my blowhose. I text the whole eatery. Garlips farts - whee? Those farts lavender this floating world. Don't mind the gap.

steve katz

Her body stutters when I say cunt against her. I taste with my hands her tendons sweating blackberry. Writing inside her with metronomes, incumbent words, typos. She said it feels like I am burrowing the word back in and she smiles with violence. My teeth seeing the rupture of her sentences all over the sheets. I lick her wounds while her legs flutter with cannibalism. Skin lashing around the words till they respire in the corners of her room. She says that they serve marrow on K street. You dig it out with a spoon. An incisor. You lick it clean with your hand inside me like a puppet. I thread her caricature body with ventriloquist strings. Isolate her dimple.clavicle.feathered eye, in a stigmata of desire. Her blood riding concealed torrents under blue brick moon. Her cunt holding light on this twisted tongue. She lets go of the word rape and it clatters like stained glass falling across the hip battered box spring. Ripping the chords that bind her desires together. She lifts with feet failing ground and opens her drought to the sound of my body pooling, with love, this warmth in her womb. My cock erasing scripture, disturbing voices ripe with weaving.

jordan okumura

to be holding kissing my way from one side of your neck to the other, hands through hair, tickling the back of your neck, tugging your head to the side so I can lick and kiss wettly...over your shoulders, dropping down.... my beard over smooth milky skin. Cupping your breasts my wet tongue upwards, taking time. Nipples in my mouth my tongue tracing around in circles   bite, kiss, flick, massage, squeeze, mouth and hands in tandem on those sexy fucking breasts

lick my way down your sides, groping, rubbing, my mouth around your belly, teasing your button, biting gently, sucking, tonguing, around your hips taste of your skin, sweet aroma, sound moaning. Hands on your hips, turn you round spanking your amazing peach of an ass, kiss your inner thighs, a tear of your juices, grab your ass and pull you tight to lap at you....running my tongue over your lips, one side then the other then agonizingly slow between them, savouring

again and again, wettly. Sliding my tongue inside wanting needing to taste all of you swirling deep inside you in circles, then figure of 8's, wettly again, faster faster upwards to your sweet swollen clit then again, again, rapid smothering tracing around it in circles.... pressure and speed.....flicking frantic up down tip of my tongue, left to right, back and forth back and forth shaking my head in tiny movements, vibrating flick, feeling your clit on my tongue loving your taste, your juice, wanting to drink you, nibbling, working my tongue around it feeling you quiver, my head back a little so just the very tip is on you fast as I can relentless flicking your hot clit fast as fuck my tongue tapping up and down as I slide two fingers inside your dripping wet delicious cunt

kylee cook

dirty, a spoon into tomato soup, sloppily spilling over the edges, pushing a saltine onto the table and blistering spots on the fingers and hands, dirty, scooping soup from the bowl with hands, dirty, searing into fingers and palms the simple mark of heat, washing down to elbows and dripping to floor, down the bare breast and abdomen to stall on skin and down and body hair, dirty,

dirty, a knife skinning a tomato, pulling off the top membrane and piling the remnants, the knife long for this sort of job, remnants pile with no skin the tomato is exposed in hands, ready to be squished into pulp, dirty, then cooked down into sauce with spices and meats added eaten with spaghetti fork twirling against large spoon, popping it into mouth and some of the ground meat drizzling out at the corners of mouth, the tongue sweeping it back in, dirty,

dirty, all is dirty, like opening small holes in the earth in a row to plant tomatoes, dirt under your nails in the creases of your palms, small mounds of dirt beside each hole amid a garden of dirt, placing the seed, the fertilizer, covering the holes of dirt with the dirt, tending to the tomatoes through rabbits and thunderstorms, thieves and pests, tending from greenness to the full red ripeness, picking them, slicing some open, fresh and juicy, sliding them down the throat, making dirty soup and sauce

jefferson hansen

## Swallow

On this doolally day I can't undo the morning,
relatch my beak and unsound the note.

My spontaneous tune trilled free and swift
left me wincing.

Kneeling face down, wearing only my freckles
I wish for wings to hide my face.

If I could unsing my naked song,
that unguarded tune, clumsy with musk,

I'd cleanse every word of my squirming desire,
reclaim each brazen syllable weighted with wanting.

Were I to breathe backwards to stop the impulse,
could I make of my longing a silent nest

so that tomorrow when that rebel bird alights on my head
I'll pluck and swallow each feather, hot and wild.

liesl jobson

My bassoon teacher lives near the park where leafless jacarandas are budding. On a bench I memorise the concerto for my audition. The notes are jittery insects scurrying across the score. My chest tightens; my belly liquefies.

I pick at a star-shaped flake of paint on the wooden slat, noodling compulsively until it slices into my nail bed. I stare at the empty tennis court, sucking my blood, awaiting my lesson.

In *Scheherazade* I fumble the flourishes. My teacher turns my chin, fingertips on my neck, saying, "Hold the pulse steady." I close my eyes. At home the passage was fluid and clean. Now my hands are clammy, contracted. He draws his chair closer, removes a leaf from my hair. He touches my temple.

"You're clenching again, Baby," he whispers, turning to the next excerpt.

My reed on my lips; the swooning *Boléro*. I play for him, wanting. He unhooks my instrument with one hand. His other circles my wrist, leading me to the corner where he stands my bassoon, stands me beside it, pressing me to the wall. He raises my skirt, reaches inside me, confirming my desire. I drop my gaze.

He leads me out into a stinking alley. Men bang pots, washing, chopping in the restaurant window. He removes my panties. Here? In the alley?

Heavy, he hurts dirty. My spine grates against the ground.

"Why here?" I ask, wanting it different.

"My girlfriend," he grunts, "might come home." He takes ages to climax.

My back is grazed. How will I hide it from my husband? Back in his studio I take up my bassoon. Dazed, I tongue my still moist reed, flexing my fingers. I can't stop thinking about how he looks. I've never seen an uncircumcised man.

He opens *The Bartered Bride*. He points and says, "Play."

liesl jobson

A drop of blood wells up, blooms in the surrounding sweat running in rivulets down the back between the hard cheeks, past the grundle down the balls, both of them slapping with a whack-whack-whack on the wet scent bottom of this well of all desire. Another and another, they swell and bloom along uneven tilled rows. The mingling smells, their species's incense, drives them to pray in this way. It is a strange thing, this particular form of perfection, this reliquary of blood, mucus, sweat and noise, this sliding of insteps along calves, this canonical closing of eyes, whispers scaling into moans. Changing positions, on hands and knees, it begins again, the next movement. Settling into a rhythm, on and on it goes, as hands rest and grab and slap, either the ass or the sheets and pillow, depending on position. A change in gravity and the bottom becomes the top, hovering for a moment before impaling the sweet spot. More gliding than riding, there is enough pleasure in this one thing to last a lifetime. But nothing but breathing and the beating of a heart lasts a lifetime. Nothing. What is needed is a change in perspective. Kisses follow the forehead, the nose, the lips, the chin, the neck, the chest, the belly, to reach that which is most wanted. Slowly at first, and then in an exponential curve, time accelerates and stops. A narrative, a reading: four eyes stare inches apart. There is a kiss, and another, and another. Spit drips in a long drool from one mouth into the other. After extended silence, words of love. "I love fucking you." "And I love fucking you."

michael harold

A woman with a nose made of butter is looking for a man with a face made of bread. On warm days when she melts, she dips Dungeness crab into the hole in her face and eats of her fate. Kissing is out of the question. Make up doesn't stick. She works in the coldest part of the french fry factory and works as much overtime as she can. When she melts, she melts alone. Summers are unbearable. She learns new languages and moves to places where it is winter, all the time dreaming of a man with a face made of bread.

greg bachar

I let you lay me down across the cold stone in the shade of a gnarled oak, limbs twisting together. The headstone reads Emma Love. Aged sixteen years. My age. Yours. Gray-green blades of grass tickle our naked legs. "Can I be your first?" If that's what you want to believe. Truth is I've dug this grave before. Died these tiny deaths. Little girl trapped in body becoming woman, becoming your woman, but not yet my woman, no not yet. As we try to learn the whole of love, Emma Love presses into my back. I imagine her cold palms pressing skyward, trying to absorb our heat through pine box, packed earth, cement slab. The weight of your body transfers my skin and blood onto the stone like a charcoal rubbing in reverse. You burn inside me, her chill seeps up from below. Scraps of poetry attach themselves to my breath and float out of my mouth in the shape of sighs. Emma's cunt lies fallow, an eternal winter in her womb and her breast and her blood. Mine is hot and slick with a million lives that will never be: never be sixteen or sixty or breathe or sigh or come.

jacqueline heffron

## Tempus es iocundum

| | |
|---|---|
| O, o, o, | Oh! Oh! Oh! |
| *totus floreo,* | I am bursting out all over! |
| *iam amore virginali* | with first love |
| *totus ardeo,* | I am burning all over! |
| *novus, novus amor est,* | New, new love is |
| *quo pereo.* | what I am dying of! |

From the *Carmina Burana*, a 13th Century manuscript containing hundreds of secular poems by monks and clerical students. The poems are mostly about sex, drinking and gambling. German composer Carl Orff set 24 of these poems to music in the 1930s.

Orff's *Carmina Burana* and the original Medieval illuminated manuscript greatly inspired the inception of this project. We highly recommend listening to Orff's cantata while reading *Dirty : Dirty.*

## About the Artist

**Mugi Takei** was born in New York and moved to Japan when her parents decided to return to their homeland. She studied painting at Massachusetts College of Art, and received her MFA from Cranbrook Academy of Art. In 2001, she traveled to Brussels, Belgium to study French, Russian history and philosophy. Two years later she moved to Kuala Lumpur, Malaysia, to live with her mother, and organize an independent film festival in support of young Japanese filmmakers and to develop cultural exchange. She served as teaching artist at the Wing Luke Museum of the Asian Pacific American Experience in Seattle, where her art is represented by Cullom Gallery.

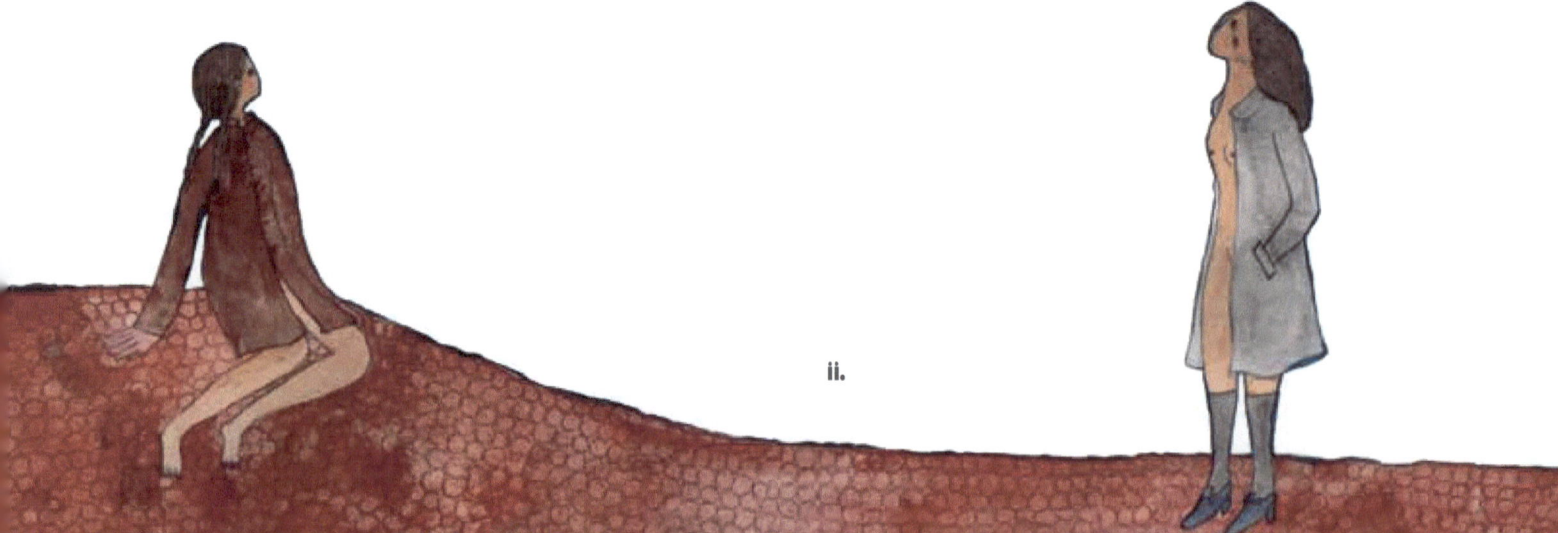

# About the Writers

**Greg Bachar** lives in Seattle. His writing has appeared previously in *Conduit, Rain Taxi, Dislocate, Bateau, Indiana Review, Sentence, Arroyo Literary Review, Quick Fiction, Southeast Review*, and *Pontoon: An Anthology of Washington State Poets*. He earned his M.F.A. in Creative Writing (Fiction) from the University of Massachusetts, Amherst.

**Elizabeth Burns** is a novelist and poet living in the Twin Cities.

**Jennifer Calkins** lives, practices evolutionary biology and writes in Seattle, Washington, where she is kept sharp and spritely by her cohabiting (smallish) primates, felids, canids and aves. Her book is *A Story of Witchery*, and she blogs at jdcalkin2001.wordpress.com and thequaildiaries.com.

**Jane L. Carman** recently received her Ph.D. from Illinois State University where she is a former Sutherland Fellow and has taught innovative writing, poetry, prose, literature, genre studies, gender in the humanities, history of women in literature, and composition among other courses. Jane is the founder of Festival of Language (found on Facebook), a series of annual readings that coincide with the Associated Writing Programs conferences.

**C. M. Connelly** lives in the Palouse of Idaho with his wife and two daughters. He enjoys long walks in the woods, general mayhem and typing words onto blank pages.

**Kylee Cook** earned her graduate degree in Creative Writing from California State University at Sacramento, and won the first Platypus Prize for Innovative College Writing. Her work appeared in *Leviathan, In Posse Review, American River Review*, and *Bellingham Review*. She served as assistant editor for Narrative Magazine and Calaveras Station and works in research at the University of California, Davis, and as a midwife's assistant.

**Beth Couture**'s writing can be found in *Drunken Boat, Gargoyle, Connotation Press--An Online Artifact, Ragazine,* and elsewhere. She is an assistant editor with Sundress Publications and a poetry editor with *Thumbnail Press.* She teaches composition at Bloomsburg University in Bloomsburg, Pennsylvania.

**Dirk Cowan** lives and works in Kansas.

**Justin Dobbs** is the author of *Billy's Room.*

**Trevor Dodge** is the author of two collections of short fiction (*Laws of Average* and *Everyone I Know Lives on Roads*), a novella (*Yellow #10*), and collaborator on the writing anti-textbook *Architectures of Possibility.* He teaches writing, literature, comics and games studies at Clackamas Community College in Oregon City and the Pacific Northwest College of Art in Portland.

**April Gigliotti** graduated from California State University at San Marcos with a BA in Literature & Writing. She enjoys living near the beach with her husband, Andrew, and beagle Eames.

**Christopher Grimes** is the author of the novel, *The Pornographers* and the novella/short story collection, *Public Works.* His award-winning short fiction has appeared in *Western Humanities Review, Beloit Fiction Journal, Reed, Cream City Review, First Intensity, Knock,* and elsewhere. He teaches literature and ficton writing at the University of Illinois at Chicago.

**Steve Halle** lives and writes in Normal, Illinois, where he is the assistant director of the English Department's Publications Unit at Illinois State University. He is the author of the poetry collection, *Map of the Hydrogen World* (Cracked Slab Books), the founding editor of the online poetry journal, *Seven Corners (7C),* and the founding director of co•im•press, a new collaborative, cooperative, immediate micropress.

**Jefferson Hansen** is the editor of AlteredScale.com and the author of *"...and beefheart saved craig."* He lives in Minneapolis.

**Michael Harold** is a poet, novelist, visual artist, information scientist and inventor. He sometimes writes under the name Michael Aro. He lives in Shreveport, Louisiana where he is the CTO of ArcMail Technology and WaLa! Solutions, as well as a co-founder of several technology startups.

**Garrett Hayes** was born in America's Heartland and makes art and solves problems all over California. Currently lives and works with his wife in Los Angeles, which treats them well.

**Jacqueline Heffron** lives and writes in California's Central Valley. She dabbles in flash fiction and pays her bills with technical writing, but her true love is the essay.

**Lily Hoang** is the author of four books, including *Unfinished*. She teaches in the MFA program at New Mexico State University.

**Eric Jeitner** is a writer and librarian. He lives in Philadelphia, a city well-regarded for its dirtiness.

**Liesl Jobson** is a Cape Town, South Africa author, photographer, editor and literary journalist. Her short story collection, *Ride theTortoise*, is forthcoming from Jacana in 2013. She is a single sculler and an ocean rower.

**Steve Katz** is considered one of the first and preeminent post-modern or avant-garde writers for notable works such as *The Exagggerations of Peter Prince* (1968), and *Saw* (1972). Other books include *Kissssss, Creamy and Delicious*, and *Swanny's Ways*, winner of the American Award in Fiction.

**Kimberly Koga** is the author of *Ligature Strain* (Tinfish Press, 2011). Her publications are included in *Lantern Review, Triton College's Ariel*, and *1913: a journal of forms*. She's currently at a small publishing office in San Diego, California.

**Stacey Levine** is the author of four books of fiction. Her recent story collection, *The Girl With Brown Fur*, was longlisted for The Story Prize and for the Washington State Book Award in 2012.

**Marilyn Jaye Lewis** is a writer of fiction, memoirs, essays, and screenplays. Among her achievements, she has written award-winning erotica for nearly a quarter of a century. In 2002, she founded the Erotic Authors Association and was at its helm until 2006.

**Robert Lopez** is the author of two novels, *Part of the World* and *Kamby Bolongo Mean River* and a collection of short fiction, *Asunder*.

**Cris Mazza** is the author of thirteen books of fiction. She is a professor and director of the Graduate Program for Writers at University of Illinois at Chicago. Her memoir, *Something Wrong With Her* is forthcoming from Jaded Ibis Press.

**Joe Milazzo** (www.slowstudies.net/jmilazzo) is the author of *The Terraces*. His writing has appeared in *H_NGM_N, The Collagist, Drunken Boat, Black Clock*, and elsewhere. Joe co-edits (with Janice Lee and Eric Lindley) the interdisciplinary arts journal *[out of nothing]* (www.outofnothing.org).

**Kathleen Miller** is a Ph.D. candidate specializing in creative writing at Illinois State University. She received her B.A. from Saint Mary's College and her M.A. from the University of Dayton. She teaches creative writing and first year composition courses.

**Nabila Najwa** lives in Indonesia where she received her BSc Medicine from Gadjah Mada University.

**Theresa O'Donnell** earned her Master's in Creative Writing and Women's and Gender Studies at Illinois State University, where she was a Sutherland Fellow. She now lives, works, and teaches her three-year-old daughter toilet humor in North Carolina. She is interested in exploring how our lumpy, wanting bodies thwart and confound social structures and likes to make the journey as entertaining as possible.

**Jordan Okumura** lives in Sacramento, California.

**Melanie Page** is a graduate of the Notre Same MFA program. She teaches Black Literature of America at St. Mary's College and at Lake Michigan College. She loves women's roller derby and has dubbed herself Professor Rage.

**M.E. Parker** is the founding editor of *Camera Obscura Journal.*

**Aimee Parkison,** Associate Professor of English at the University of North Carolina at Charlotte, has received a Christopher Isherwood Fellowship, a Writers at Work Fellowship, a Kurt Vonnegut Fiction Prize, and an American Antiquarian Society fellowship for research related to a historical novel-in-progress. Her book, *The Innocent Party*, was published by BOA Editions' American Reader Series in 2012. Her story collection, *Woman with Dark Horses*, won the first annual Starcherone Fiction Prize.

**AE Reiff** translated the letters from Kurk Wold's numerical code palimpsest of the *Mouser Airpark* with its eight and more unfathomed levels in the Distortion Dome of air.

**J. M. Rees** is an architect, writer, and visual artist. He is principal of Jack Rees Interiors in Kansas City, Missouri.

**Doug Rice** is the author of *Between Appear and Disappear* (forthcoming from Jaded Ibis Press), *Dream Memoirs of a Fabulist*, *Blood of Mugwump* (selected by Kathy Acker as the runner-up FC2 Best First Novel Award), *A Good Cuntboy is Hard to Find* and *Skin Prayer: fragments of abject memory.*

**Thaddeus Rutkowski** is the author of the innovative novels *Haywire, Tetched* and *Roughhouse*. He teaches literature at City University of New York and fiction writing at the Writer's Voice of the West Side YMCA in Manhattan.

**Heather Hendix Russell** is a Video Production Specialist for a Midwest university. With an interdisciplinary arts education from the Kansas City Art Institute, she utilizes her diverse skills to help facilitate distance education, create graphic designs for websites, and paint, sew and write.

**Davis Schneiderman**'s novel, *DRAIN*, often uses the word c_nt. davisschneiderman.com.

**Mikal Shapiro** is is producer of the TV show, *Go! Go! Global Girls*, and a graduate of The School of the Art Institute of Chicago Film Video New Media and Animation.

**Gary J. Shipley** is the author of six books of various sizes. His work has appeared recently or is forthcoming in *The Black Herald, Gargoyle, nthposition, elimae, >kill author, 3:AM*, and others. More details can be found at www.garyjshipley.blogspot.co.uk.

**Ascot J. Smith** is a filmmaker, writer, and installation artist. He creates genre-influenced narratives that primarily focus on coming of age and the consequences of a prolonged adolescence. Smith's stories are presented through multiple mediums and reflect an influence of science-fiction stories and growing up in the Midwest.

**Rob Stephenson** is an inter-media artist (author, composer, visual artist). He has been creating texts, music, video, films, paintings, drawings, and installations for over thirty years. He is author of the novel, *Passes Through*, and co-edited the anthology *Tough Guys* with Bill Brent.

**Helen Tran** is an artist, writer, photographer and aspiring filmmaker.

**J. A. Tyler** is the author of *Inconceivable Wilson, A Man of Glass & All the Ways We Have Failed, A Shiny, Unused Heart*, and *Girl With Oars & Man Dying*. His work has appeared in *Black Warrior Review, Diagram, New York Tyrant*, and elsewhere. He is founding editor of Mud Luscious Press.

**c.vance** is the author of the novel, *We: A Reimagined Family History*. He enjoys writing dirty little stories.

**Laura Vena** is a writer, artist, curator and translator whose work has appeared in *Super Arrow, Tarpaulin Sky, In Posse Review, Antennae* and elsewhere. She holds an MFA in Creative Writing from CalArts, coordinates literary events for Avenue 50 Studio in Highland Park, and is co-founder of the interdisciplinary arts organization, Strophe, at http://schoolofstrophe.com.

**Dennis Weiser** is the author of a more than a dozen works of prose and poetry, including a Beautiful Lies and Crash Dummies. He is currently writing Sirens and Sleepwalkers, a crime novel set in present day Kansas City, Missouri.

**Hal Wert** is a Professor of Literature and History at the Kansas City Art institute where his courses include the Modern Japanese Novel and the Tale of Genji. He is currently working on a novel, a fictional biography of Tad Waller, constructed randomly through Tad's memory in flash fiction vignettes.

**Lane Williams** is an artist and writer whose works include *Acknowledge and Proceed*, *The Ultimate Guide to Cool*, and *This is a World*. He lives in Chicago, Illinois.

**Alyssa Wisener** lives/plays in Fresno, California. She has an undergraduate degree in English from CSU Fresno, numerous furbabies, and a most wonderful "partner-in-crimae."

**Rion Woolf** writes erotic fiction and teaches at a Midwestern college.

**Lidia Yuknavitch** is the author of *The Chronology of Water* and *Dora: A Headcase* and some stuff coming up.

Write your own dirty words.

Draw your own dirty pictures.

Write your own dirty words.

Draw your own dirty pictures.

XV.

www.ingramcontent.com/pod-product-compliance
Lightning Source LLC
Chambersburg PA
CBHW041134100726
47911CB00003B/121